IF EVER YOU GO TO DUBLIN TOWN

A historic guide to the city's street names

CAROL & JONATHAN BARDON

General Post Office, O'Connell Street

THE
BLACKSTAFF
PRESS
BELFAST AND WOLFEBORO, NEW HAMPSHIRE

First published in 1988 by
The Blackstaff Press Limited
3 Galway Park, Dundonald, Belfast BT16 0AN, Northern Ireland
and
27 South Main Street, Wolfeboro, New Hampshire 03894 USA

Printed by The Guernsey Press Limited

British Library Cataloguing in Publication Data
Bardon, Carol
If ever you go to Dublin town: a
historic guide to the city's street names.
1. Dublin. Street names
I. Title II. Bardon, Jonathan
914.18'35'0014

Library of Congress Cataloging-in-Publication Data
Bardon, Carol, 1942–
If ever you go to Dublin town.
1. Street names — Ireland — Dublin (Dublin) — Dictionaries.
2. Dublin (Dublin) — History — Dictionaries.
3. Historic sites — Ireland — Dublin (Dublin) — Dictionaries.
I. Bardon, Jonathan, 1941– . II. Title.
DA995.D75B37 1988 941.8'35'00321 88–5012

ISBN 0-85640-397-0

Carol Bardon was born in Belfast in 1942 and she graduated from Queen's University in 1963. She received her Diploma of Education in 1964 and then taught English for nine years. She has worked as a sailing instructor and is at present employed as a part-time library assistant at Queen's University and as a part-time teacher of English at the College of Business Studies in Belfast.

Jonathan Bardon was born in Dublin in 1941 and was educated at the High School Dublin, at Trinity College Dublin, and at Queen's University Belfast. He has lived in Belfast since 1963, and is Head of the Department of Academic and Continuing Education at the College of Business Studies. He has written local history articles for the *Sunday News*, and from 1975 to 1980 he was scriptwriter for the much-praised BBC schools broadcasts series, *Modern Irish History*. In addition, he published in 1970 a school textbook, *The Struggle for Ireland: AD 400 to AD 1450*, in 1982 *Belfast: An Illustrated History*, in 1984 *Dublin: One Thousand Years of Wood Quay* and in 1985 *Belfast: 1000 Years*.

for Charlotte,
Barbara and Carol

If ever you go to Dublin town
In a hundred years or so
Inquire for me in Baggot Street
And what I was like to know. . .

from 'If Ever You Go To Dublin Town'
Patrick Kavanagh

CONTENTS

COLLEGE GREEN

INTRODUCTION

The heart of Dublin is lively and bustling, welcoming citizen and tourist alike with its friendly pubs, fashionable shops, hawkers' stalls, garish fast-food bars and up-market restaurants. It is a city of contrasts. Tall, angular office blocks – to some a celebration of modernism and progress, to others abominations – rub shoulders with gracious Georgian houses, some restored to their original elegance while others, crumbling into ruin, remind us of the tenement slums which are the setting for Sean O'Casey's plays.

The contrasting faces of Dublin hint at its tumultuous history. Street names, strange in a modern context, lead us into its past – Bull Alley, Weaver's Square, Golden Lane, Mary's Abbey and Fishamble Street. Some names are not as straightforward as they seem: Hammond Lane, for example, takes on a sinister glamour when we discover it was originally Hangman Lane. Names of viceroys – agents of British colonial domination – like Grafton, Capel and Camden, jostle indiscriminately with those of Irish patriots like Oliver Bond, Lord Edward, Sean Mac Dermott and Cathal Brugha. Some names are ecclesiastical like Whitefriars, Kevin, Patrick and Thomas while others are frankly profane like Winetavern, Fumbally and Copper. Some streets preserve the names of property developers who showed that building for profit was not incompatible with aesthetic sensibility such as Gardiner, Molesworth, Ely, Leeson and Hatch – how many modern speculators will be remembered with equal gratitude? And some names, such as Wood Quay, have their origins in the infancy of the city.

The core of old Dublin lies between Áth Cliath, the hurdle ford just upstream of the present Father Matthew Bridge, and Dubhlinn, the dark pool formed where the Poddle Stream met the River Liffey which is now the gardens of Dublin Castle. Only when Dubliners learned of the uniquely rich finds made by archaeologists in the 1960s and 1970s, did they become fully aware of the antiquity and historic importance of their city. Impressive evidence of dense Viking settlement was uncovered in High Street, Winetavern Street and Fishamble Street – streets which have preserved the location of the city's first thoroughfares. Dublin clearly was one of the most flourishing cities in the Viking world. The city's mixed Hiberno-Norse population became Christian, and Sitric Silkenbeard, King of Dublin, built Christ Church Cathedral overlooking Dubhghall's Bridge erected adjacent to the hurdle ford.

When the Normans invaded Ireland they found Dubliners their most tenacious adversaries. However, the city fell to them in 1170 and Henry II, King of England and Angevin Emperor, made Dublin the capital of his Irish Lordship, granting it to the citizens of Bristol. For the next 700 years and more Dublin was to be the centre of English rule in Ireland. King John came to the city in 1210 and there saw Dublin Castle close to completion as one of the mightiest bastions in the land.

The Northmen, now known as Ostmen, crossed to the north side of the Liffey to begin the settlement later named Oxmantown, around St Michan's Church. The walls of the city were extended and strengthened, pierced by guarded gateways. Suburbs developed in the Liberties beyond the walls, so named because citizens dwelling there were free of taxes imposed within the walls. The tidal pool of Dubhlinn was dammed, thus giving Dame Street its name; the foreshore by Christ Church Cathedral was built out into the river to make an anchorage – Wood Quay; foreign merchants refreshed themselves in Winetavern Street; and some streets, such as Crockers' Street named after the crockers or potters, recorded the dwelling places of artisans.

Plague, famine, endless wars and the decline of English power in Ireland halted Dublin's growth until the late sixteenth century when the city assumed a new importance as the focal point for the Elizabethan reconquest of the country. Trinity College was founded on the site of the Priory of All Hallows. In the seventeenth century Dublin grew rapidly: the quays were extended downstream; great landowners, such as the Earl of Cork, erected town houses in the city centre; and Sir Humphrey Jervis began the development of the city north of the river. In the long era of calm following William III's victories, Dublin became one of the great cities of Europe, and within the British Empire, second in size only to London.

In 1750 Dublin's population had reached around 130,000 and the city extended rapidly outwards. The Gardiner family built dignified rows of red-brick houses north of the Liffey and made Sackville Street (now O'Connell Street) the most fashionable quarter in Dublin. South-east of the river, Viscount Molesworth laid out his land in building plots; one of these was bought by the Earl of Kildare who engaged Richard Cassels to design Leinster House. As the social standing of the area was immediately enhanced, other elegant streets were laid out in the vicinity by Joshua Dawson, the Leeson family and Lord Fitzwilliam of Meryon.

Legislative independence, won in 1782, inaugurated the most magnificent era in Dublin's history. Great public buildings were built or extended; the erection of Carlisle Bridge pushed the city's centre of gravity further east; and the Wide Street Commissioners laid out thoroughfares such as D'Olier Street and Westmoreland Street. But Ireland was a place of contradictions: following a furious rebellion in 1798, the British government cajoled the Irish Parliament into voting itself out of existence in 1800. Steady decline followed the Union: the gentry sold their town houses, and the hand-loom weavers of the Liberties faced destitution. The middle classes moved out to the townships of Pembroke, Rathmines and Rathgar, and the noble Georgian terraces became overcrowded tenements for the poor. And in 1891 Dublin had the ignominy of being overtaken by Belfast as Ireland's largest city.

The years from 1914 brought rapid change as in many other European capitals. While suppressing the insurrection of Easter 1916, government forces destroyed much of Sackville Street and other streets in the vicinity. In the Troubles that followed the Custom House and the Four Courts were burned and sections of central Dublin were levelled. Neglect, shortage of money and neutrality during the Second World War ensured the preservation – in a somewhat decayed condition – of a great deal of Georgian Dublin. It was not until the late 1950s that a surge of economic growth brought a long-sought improvement in the living conditions of Dublin's citizens. In the haste of change a dreadful tastelessness prevailed. Some of Georgian Dublin had advanced too far in decay to be worthy of preservation, but there was much wanton destruction. Dublin Corporation's determination to build its new offices on Wood Quay led to the eradication of historical evidence on an unprecedented scale – to the acute dismay of scholars across Europe. Recent tasteful and homely domestic architecture in the city centre shows the city fathers' belated penitence and seems to indicate a new sensitivity to the city's remarkable past.

This book is not a street directory but is intended as a pocket guide to the most historic and interesting of Dublin's streets. It cannot, therefore, describe every street and concentrates on those confined within the North and South Circular Roads.

The authors would like to express their thanks to Mary Clark of the Dublin Corporation Archives in the City Hall; Revd Brendan Haythornthwaite; Kieran Fagan; Richard Hawkins; and Sandra Carinduff.

Carol and Jonathan Bardon, 1988

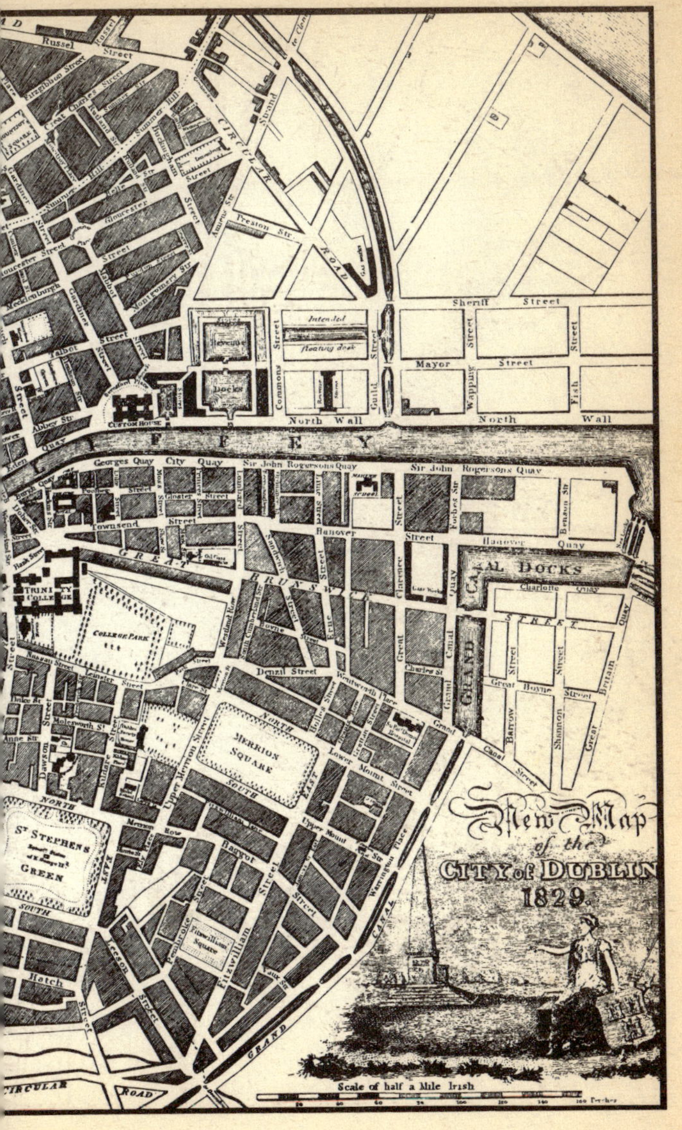

New Map
of the
CITY of DUBLIN
1829.
Scale of half a Mile Irish
Perches
Russel Street
Fitzgibbon Street
Great Charles Street
Summer Hill
Gloucester Street
Circular Road
Strand
Preston Str.
Amiens Str
Talbot Street
Montgomery Str
Mecklenburgh
Gardiner Street
Intended floating dock
Revenue
Docks
Custom House
Commons Street
Guild Street
Sheriff Street
Mayor Street
Wapping Street
Fish Street
North Wall
Abbey Str
Eden Quay
F F E Y
Georges Quay
City Quay
Sir John Rogersons Quay
Moss Street
Gloster Street
Townsend Street
Lombard Street
Hanover Street
Forbes Str
Benson Str
Hanover Quay
Canal Docks
Charlotte Quay
Great Brunswick Street
Trinity College
College Park
Westland Row
Denzil Street
Wentworth Place
Grand Canal
Charles St
Great Boyne Street
Barrow Street
Shannon Street
Great Britain Quay
Canal Street
Nassau Street
Leinster Street
Duke St
Dawson Street
Molesworth St
Anne Str
Kildare Street
Merrion Square
North
South
East
Lower Mount Street
Upper Mount Street
Upper Merrion Street
Baggot Street
Warrington Place
St Stephens Green
Fitzwilliam Square
Pembroke Street
Fitzwilliam Street
Leeson Street
Hatch Street
Circular Road

ROYAL HIBERNIAN ACADEMY

ABBEY STREET
off O'Connell Street

After St Mary's Abbey, founded by the Vikings and later taken over by the Cistercians. Though severely damaged by fire in 1304 and its tower demolished to strengthen the city walls in 1317, it was the richest religious house in the late medieval Pale and probably in the whole country. It was here that Silken Thomas, son of the imprisoned viceroy Garret Óg Fitzgerald, threw down the sword of state and began his ill-fated rebellion in June 1534. Only part of the chapter house remains on the site bounded by Capel Street, Mary's Abbey, Mary Street Little and Arran Street.

Abbey Street runs through the once extensive Liberty of St Mary. The Mechanics' Institute, an early centre of the Gaelic Revival, became the Abbey Theatre in 1904. The building (then at 27 Lower Abbey Street) was demolished after a fire in July 1951. The new theatre was opened at another site in the street in 1966. The street was much damaged by artillery fire in 1916 during the Easter Rising.

Called Abbey Street in 1728

See also the Liberties, Jervis Street, Mary's Abbey *and* Mary Street

AMIENS STREET

After Edward Stratford, Viscount Amiens, 2nd Earl of Aldborough. He built a sumptuous mansion close by, adjacent to the Royal Canal, in 1796. The railway terminus for the Great Northern Railway was put up here in 1846.

Charles Lever, the novelist, was born in one of the houses knocked down to make way for the station. In 1966, to commemorate the fiftieth anniversary of the Easter Rising, the name was changed to Connolly Station. Aldborough House became first a school, then a barrack and finally a store for the Post Office.

Called Amiens Street in 1829

ANGLESEA STREET
off Dame Street

After Arthur Annesley, 1st Earl of Anglesea. He had a house on College Green and owned land between Dame Street and the River Liffey during the reign of Charles II. Who actually had title to the estate when the street was built was the subject of one of the most celebrated Irish law cases which dragged on for decades. The wicked uncle, Richard Annesley, had his nephew, a rival claimant to the inheritance, shanghaied and sold as a slave in Virginia, and kept control until his death in 1761.

Called Anglesea Street in 1728

ANNE STREET
off Grafton Street

After St Anne's Church, designed by Isaac Wells, in Dawson Street. Built in 1707 in the reign of Queen Anne, it paid homage to powers both secular and spiritual.

Called Anne Street in 1723

ARDEE STREET
off The Coombe

After Sir Edward Brabazon, Baron Ardee, father of the first of the Earls of Meath. In July 1539, during the dissolution of the monasteries, Henry VIII's under-treasurer William Brabazon acquired the Abbey of St Thomas and its extensive liberty which soon became known as the Liberty of the Earl of Meath. The area was developed over the next three centuries by the Brabazons as a new home for English and Continental Protestant weavers. The weavers sometimes clashed bloodily with Catholic butchers from the Ormonde Market and they often supported radical causes: invading the Irish Commons in 1759; joining combinations in the 1770s; becoming United Irishmen in 1798; and following the revolutionary leader Robert Emmet in 1803. The Protestant character of the area did not last beyond the eighteenth century and acute economic depression set in after 1815. Formerly called Crooked Staff.

Called Ardee Street in 1792

See also Brabazon Row, Chamber Street, Earl Street *and* Meath Street

STEEVENS'S HOSPITAL

ASTON QUAY

After Henry Aston, merchant. He appears in 1710 as a trustee of the will of Dr Richard Steevens who founded the hospital which bears his name.

In 1756 it included the present Burgh Quay and extended as far as Hawkins Street.

This was a principal landing place for coal and salt.

Called Aston Quay in 1708

AUBURN STREET
off Fontenoy Street

After the name of Oliver Goldsmith's *Deserted Village:*

> Sweet Auburn, loveliest village of the plain,
> Where health and plenty cheared the labouring swain. . .
> Amidst thy bowers the tyrant's hand is seen,
> And desolation saddens all thy green. . .
> And trembling, shrinking from the spoiler's hand,
> Far, far away, thy children leave the land.
> Ill fares the land, to hastening ills a prey,
> Where wealth accumulates and men decay. . .

Called Auburn Street in 1878

AUNGIER STREET
joins South Great George's Street

After Sir Francis Aungier, James I's Master of the Rolls. He acquired the Whitefriars' Abbey lands between the old city walls and St Stephen's Green. This street was part of a major building development by a later Sir Francis Aungier, created Earl of Longford in 1677, which included Longford Street and Cuffe Street.

The poet Thomas Moore was born in number 12, a house in the Dutch Billy style which

INTERIOR OF CARMELITE PRIORY

remained intact until the early twentieth century.

A fifteenth-century wooden statue, *Our Lady of Dublin,* from St Mary's Abbey is kept in the Carmelite priory here.

Called Aungier Street in 1670

See also Cuffe Street

BACHELOR'S WALK

Not a beaux walk but after an early-eighteenth-century property owner called Batchelor. After an attempt to confiscate illegal German arms, the King's Own Scottish Borderers opened fire on a jeering crowd of supporters of the National Volunteers here on the eve of the First World War in July 1914. Three civilians were killed.

Called Bachelor's Walk in 1728

BACK LANE
off Cornmarket

After its position behind or at the *back* of High

Street. The simplicity of its name gives an indication of its antiquity, suggesting that it was commonly described thus before it was even officially a street.

A Jesuit refuge in the seventeenth century. The Tailors' Hall is the street's most noted building, recently restored. Here the guilds met; the United Irishmen held their early debates; the Catholic Convention met in 1792 and the Repealers called for an end to the Union in the 1840s.

Called Back Lane in 1610

BAGGOT STREET

Formerly Baggotrath, after the Manor of the Rath granted to Robert Bagod in the thirteenth century. A decisive victory here in 1649 by the Parliamentarians, led by Colonel Michael Jones, over Ormonde's Royalists, ensured a safe landing for Cromwell and his Ironsides. Lower Baggot Street was called Gallows Road in the eighteenth century. The founder of Young Ireland, Thomas Davis (1814–45), lived at number 67 and John and Henry Sheares, two United Irish conspirators executed in 1798, lived in number 128.

Called Baggot Street in 1773

See also Mespil Road *and* Whitefriars Street

BERESFORD PLACE
off Eden Quay

After John Beresford, First Commissioner of the Revenue and the Younger Pitt's fixer in the Irish Parliament. He arranged the building of the Custom House and the demise of Grattan's Parliament.

Called Beresford Place in 1791

See also Eden Quay *and* Marlborough Street

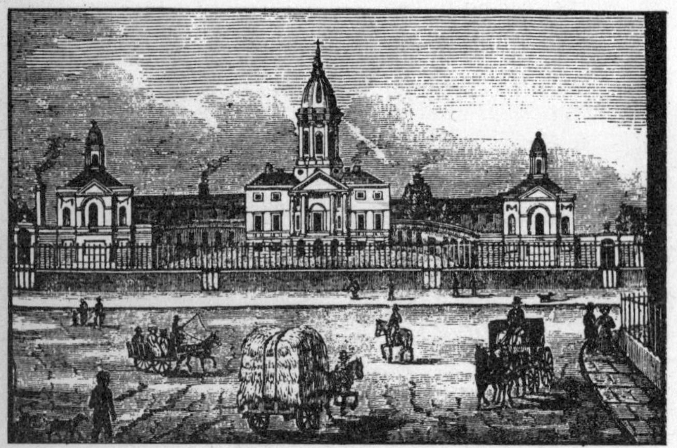

BLEW-COAT SCHOOL

BLACKHALL PLACE
joins Stoneybatter

After Sir Thomas Blackhall, Lord Mayor in 1769 and chairman of the committee which rebuilt King's Hospital in the 1770s. Founded in 1672 as the Blew-Coat School, King's Hospital is a fine example of Thomas Ivory's architectural skill. Known as Blackhall Market in the late eighteenth century. Like Blackhall Street, this was laid over the last part of Oxmantown Green.

Called Blackhall Place in 1822

See also Smithfield

BLACKHALL STREET *see* Blackhall Place

BLESSINGTON STREET
off Dorset Street

After the 1st Earl of Blessington, eldest son of the second Luke Gardiner, Lord Mountjoy.

Called Blessington Street in 1795

See also Gardiner Street *and* Mountjoy Square

BOLTON STREET
off Capel Street

After Sir Charles Powlett, 7th Marquis of Winchester and 2nd Duke of Bolton. Several times a Lord Justice (ruling in the absence of the viceroy) and Lord Lieutenant 1717–19. Celebrated for its technical college.

Called Bolton Street in 1724

BONHAM STREET
off Watling Street

After Alderman Bonham, a hide merchant

Called Bonham Street in 1792

BOW LANE, EAST
off Aungier Street

A corruption of the medieval name Elbow Lane, descriptive of its shape.

Called Bow Lane, East in 1728

BOW STREET
off King Street, North

After John, Baron Bowes, Lord Chancellor in

1761. He lived here in a house which later became the Night Asylum.

Called Bow Street in 1728

BRABAZON ROW
off The Coombe

After the surname of the Earls of Meath. Originally called Cuckold's Row, 1756.

Called Brabazon Street in 1766 and Row in 1775

See also Ardee Street

BRICKFIELD LANE
off Cork Street

Probably so called because it supplied clay for brick-making.

Called Brickfield Lane in 1756

BRIDE STREET
meets Chancery Lane

After the Church of St Brigid mentioned in 1178. One of the finest houses, number 36, was owned by an apothecary named Patrick Bride but this has no bearing on the street's name.

Called Bride Street in 1465

BRIDGE STREET
off Merchants' Quay

After the Old Bridge built by King John in 1210 and rebuilt by the Dominicans in 1385. Rebuilt in 1818 and renamed Whitworth Bridge after Charles, Earl of Whitworth, Lord Lieutenant 1813–17. Renamed again *c.* 1938 as Father

Matthew Bridge, after the leader of the nineteenth-century Irish temperance movement.

The Leinster Directory of the United Irishmen was arrested by Town Major Charles Henry Sirr in Oliver Bond's house (number 9) on 12 March 1798. Nearly opposite, in a narrow court on the western side, is Dublin's oldest tavern, the Brazen Head.

Called Bridge Street in 1317

See also Oliver Bond Street

BRIDGEFOOT STREET
off Usher's Quay

After the name of Sir William Ussher's house which was at the foot of the Old Bridge. Originally and picturesquely named Dirty Lane. The scene of conspiracy during the 1803 rising led by Robert Emmet.

Called Bridgefoot Street in 1732

BROADSTONE STATION

BROADSTONE
off Phibsborough Road

Built by the Midland Great Western Railway in

1879 as an approach to Broadstone Station. Called Broadstone in 1756

BROWN STREET *see* Tenterfields

BRUNSWICK STREET, NORTH
meets Stoneybatter

Formerly Channel Row, possibly because water was brought through here from the adjacent Bradogue river. The name, presumably, is in honour of the Hanoverian ruling house.

Called Brunswick Street, North in 1766

BULL ALLEY
off Patrick Street

A notorious slum cleared at the turn of the century. The original city wall passed through Cornmarket, Bull Alley and Golden Lane and portions of it are still embedded in the streets. The proximity of Ship Street, that is, Sheep Street, suggests that there could have been a livestock market in this area or perhaps that this was originally pasture land. The medieval bullring, where bulls were baited, was probably in this vicinity.

Called Bull Alley in 1680

See also Golden Lane, Greek Street *and* Ship Street

BURGH QUAY

After Elizabeth Burgh, mother of John Foster, the last Speaker of the Irish Parliament.

Called Burgh Quay in 1809

See also Foster Place *and* Oriel Street

CAMDEN STREET
joins Wexford Street

Probably named after John Pratt, 2nd Earl of Camden. The street was built in 1778, though Camden did not begin his disastrous viceroyalty until 1795. Originally the southern end of the medieval Whitefriars Lane.

Called Camden Street in 1778

CAPEL STREET

Built by Sir Humphrey Jervis and named by him after Arthur Capel, Earl of Essex, Lord Lieutenant 1672–7. Sent to the Tower for conspiring with Monmouth, Essex was found there with his throat cut in July 1683. The principal thoroughfare north of the city until supplanted by Sackville [O'Connell] Street.

Called Capel Street in 1697

See also Essex Quay *and* Essex Street, West

CARMAN'S HALL
off Spitalfields

Probably after carmen who had the unpleasant but essential task of carting animal dung and the contents of cesspits out beyond the city limits. The Assembly Rolls record fines of 11d. and 12d. to be imposed on carmen who dumped the contents of their vehicles within the city walls.

Called Carman's Hall in 1756

DUBLIN CASTLE

CASTLE STREET
joins Cork Hill

After the castle of Dublin. Recorded as *vicus castri*, 'the way to the castle', in 1235. Fronting Dublin Castle, the heart of English rule in Ireland for some seven centuries, it was traversed by many rulers including John, Richard II, James II, William III, George IV, Victoria and Edward VII. Apart from Dublin Castle, the most distinguished building is probably La Touche Bank, built about 1730, though much of it was removed in 1945. The La Touche family played a leading role in setting up the Bank of Ireland.

Called Castle Street in 1235

CATHAL BRUGHA STREET
off O'Connell Street

After the celebrated insurgent leader in 1916, who later became President of Sinn Féin and was killed in a shoot-out with Free State troops in 1922 close to the street named after him. Originally Gregg's Lane, renamed Findlater's Place in 1882 after the wine merchant and grocer, William Findlater.

Called Cathal Brugha Street *c.* 1933

CATHEDRAL LANE
off Kevin Street, Upper

Adjacent to St Patrick's Cathedral. Formerly Cabbage Garden Lane which led to a burial ground.

Called Cathedral Lane in 1792

CHAMBER STREET
off Ardee Street

Originally Chambré Street, after a family connection of the Earls of Meath. Dutch Billy houses survived here until the 1950s.

Called Chamber Street in 1728

See also Ardee Street

CHANCERY LANE
off Bride Street

So called because lawyers lived here before the Four Courts were transferred to the north side of the River Liffey in the 1780s.

Called Chancery Lane in 1728

CHANCERY PLACE
off Inns Quay

After the Court of Chancery, one of the adjacent Four Courts.

Called Chancery Place in 1834

See also Inns Quay

CHARLEMONT STREET
off Harcourt Road

After James Caulfield, 1st Earl of Charlemont (1728–99), art collector, poetaster, extravagant builder, Volunteer Commander-in-Chief, and leader of the Patriots in the Irish House of Lords.

Called Charlemont Street in 1789

See also Parnell Square

CHATHAM STREET
off Grafton Street

After William Pitt, 1st Earl of Chatham, possibly to flatter his son who had become Prime Minister in 1783.

Called Chatham Street in 1785

CHRISTCHURCH PLACE
joins High Street

After Christ Church Cathedral founded by the Vikings in 1038. Formerly Skinners' Row as the men who prepared skins for tanning worked here in medieval times. The old fleshambles were nearby, just east of Fishamble Street. The medieval town hall, or Tholsel,

CHRIST CHURCH CATHEDRAL

stood at the corner of Skinners' Row and Nicholas Street. Built in the reign of Edward II, rebuilt in 1683 and 1783, it was pulled down in 1809. Carberie House, on the south side of the street, was the town house of the Earls of Kildare until it became Dick's Coffee House, from which *Pue's Occurrences,* Ireland's first regular newspaper, was published.

Previously Bothe Street in 1305, after booths set up by traders next the cathedral. First recorded as *vicus pellipariorum,* 'Pelt Street', in 1284.

Called Christchurch Place in 1833

CHURCH STREET
off Arran Quay

After St Michan's, once the Viking parish church, now famous for its Georgian woodcarving, Wolfe Tone's death mask, Handel's organ and dry vaults, where (until recently) 'crusaders'' hands could be shaken.

ST MICHAN'S CHURCH

On Tuesday evening, 2 September 1913, two houses collapsed in this street. The sixteen rooms above the shops were occupied by ten families – over forty people. Seven people were killed and many more severely injured. A committee of inquiry reported the following year that 87,305 people lived in similar tenement houses and that 80 per cent of these families occupied only one room each.

Called Church Street in 1610

See also St Michan's Street

CITY QUAY

So called because the Dublin Corporation paid for this quay to fill a gap between George's Quay and Sir John Rogerson's Quay.

Called City Quay in 1766

CLARE STREET
off Merrion Square

After John Holles, 1st Earl of Clare (in Suffolk – English peerage), whose daughter married the eighteenth-century property developer, Oliver, 2nd Viscount Fitzwilliam of Meryon. Not to be confused with John Fitzgibbon ('Black Jack'), 1st Earl of Clare (Irish peerage), Lord Chancellor at the time of the Union.

Called Clare Street in 1762

See also Holles Street

CLARENDON STREET
off Wicklow Street

After Henry Hyde, 2nd Earl of Clarendon, brother-in-law to James II and Lord Lieutenant 1685–6; he grew asparagus and found Dublin Castle 'the worst and most inconvenient lodging in the world'.

Called Clarendon Street in 1728

CLONMEL STREET
off Harcourt Street

After 'Copper-faced' John Scott, 1st Earl of Clonmell, Irish Attorney-General and Chief Justice of the King's Bench in Ireland, notorious for his bullying tone and political opportunism.

Called Clonmel Street in 1839

See also Earlsfort Terrace

COLERAINE STREET
off King Street, North

After the Ulster linen town

Called Coleraine Street in 1756

See also Linenhall Street

TRINITY COLLEGE

COLLEGE GREEN

After Trinity College, founded in 1591. Originally Hoggen Green after *hauges* (Viking burial mounds) which in turn named the Augustinian nunnery of St Mary de Hogges which stood on the Green and served as a place of retirement for elderly nuns of good class.

BANK OF IRELAND

Most of the Green served as common pasture for the city. Here, until late-Elizabethan times, there were archery butts, a bowling alley, a public gallows and outdoor plays.

Now the thoroughfare is flanked by Trinity College façade (1759) and the Parliament House (begun in 1729, and today the Bank of Ireland). Scene of the great Volunteer demonstration of 4 November 1779 and site of the equestrian statue of William III (blown up 1836, repaired, and blown up again in 1929).

The university library is the most important in the country and includes in its collection the Book of Kells, the Book of Durrow, the Book of Dimma, the Book of Leinster and the Book of Armagh.

Called College Green in 1666

See also Temple Lane

COMMONS STREET
off North Wall

So called possibly in recognition of the financial help given by the Irish House of Commons in the construction of the North Wall.

Called Commons Street in 1773

CONSTITUTION HILL
joins Church Street, Upper

After the 'constitution of 1782' which celebrated Grattan's Parliament.

Previously known as Glasmanoge, then Townsend Street North after George Townshend, 1st Marquis of Townshend, Lord Lieutenant 1767–72. Lord Chancellor 'Black Jack' Fitzgibbon drew a pistol on a mob here in 1795 and claimed to have dispersed it single-handed.

Called Constitution Hill in 1792

See also Ely Place

COOK STREET
off Bridge Street

Originally Cooks' Street after the Guild of Cooks who lived here.

Called Cook Street in 1270

THE COOMBE

First mentioned in the fifteenth century and named after the hollow created by the flow of the Poddle Stream. The centre of the city's silk and wool hand-loom weaving trade and noted for the political radicalism of its journeymen. 'Biddy Mulligan' was, according to the song, the pride of it.

Called The Coombe in 1454

See also Tenterfields *and* Weaver's Square

COPE STREET
off Anglesea Street

After Robert Cope of Loughgall, Co. Armagh. He married into the Fownes family (which gave its name to the adjacent street).

Called Cope Street in 1756

See also Fownes Street

COPPER ALLEY
off Fishamble Street

After the copper money coined and issued here by Lady Alice, widow of Sir Geoffrey Fenton, Irish Secretary of State.

Called Copper Alley in 1705

CORK HILL
meets Dame Street

After Cork House, a great mansion built on the site of the Church of St Mary del Dam by Richard Boyle, 1st Earl of Cork. An Elizabethan–Jacobean adventurer, he became immensely wealthy after acquiring Sir Walter Raleigh's Munster lands for £1,000.

The 'Hell-fire Club', notorious for drinking, wenching and practising the black arts, was founded here in the Eagle Tavern in 1735 by the 1st Earl of Rosse. Lucas's Coffee House

OFFICE OF THE CITY TREASURER

was notorious for its duels. These buildings were swept away to build the Royal Exchange, completed in 1779 and now the City Hall. The gold S-collar presented by William III to the Lord Mayor, and the municipal archives going back to the twelfth century, are preserved here.

Called Cork Hill in 1658

See also Dame Street *and* Exchange Street

CORK STREET
joins Dolphin's Barn

Probably after a member of the Boyle family (the Earls of Cork) rather than the capital city of Munster. Considered part of the area of the Coombe, the street was a centre of fine wool and silk hand-loom weaving and one of Ireland's first cotton factories flourished here for a time.

Called Cork Street in 1728

See also Tenterfields

CORNMARKET
joins High Street

Since 1863 has incorporated Cutpurse Row

and Keysar's Lane. The latter, according to Richard Stanihurst, is a corruption of Kiss Arse Lane where, in the frost, citizens often did 'clinke their bums' on the cobbles – the Victorian Sir John Gilbert was too embarrassed to transcribe this explanation unaltered.

Outside the west gate was the main market for corn, hay and straw in medieval and Tudor times and marketplaces were – and still are – a favourite haunt for cutpurses and pickpockets.

In the seventeenth century prisoners were kept here in cages before being transported to the West Indies. Partly swept away by street widening in the 1970s.

Called Cornmarket in 1612

CRAMPTON COURT
off Dame Street

Built by Philip Crampton, Lord Mayor 1758–9 and bookseller. Carved doors were demolished in the 1960s. Also Crampton Quay, 1766.

Called Crampton Court *c.* 1740

CRAMPTON QUAY *see* Crampton Court

CROKER LANE
off Marshalsea Lane

Recorded as Crockers' Street in 1263

Called Croker Lane in 1590

See also Oliver Bond Street

CROMWELL'S QUARTERS
off James's Street

After Oliver Cromwell, perhaps in an attempt by the Dublin Corporation to promote Puritan virtue or a fear of Draconian discipline among its inhabitants as it was originally named Murdering Lane in 1603. The now defunct Cutthroat Lane (1756) off Mount Brown was renamed Roundhead Row at the same time. A dangerous area, it seems.

Called Cromwell's Quarters in 1876

CROW STREET
off Dame Street

After William Crow, appointed Chirographer and Chief Prothonotary to the Court of Common Pleas in 1597.

William Petty, who came to Ireland in 1653 as a doctor in Cromwell's army, worked on the redistribution of forfeited lands in a house here called the Crow's Nest which was also the meeting place of the Dublin Philosophical Society. The opening of the Crow Street Theatre in October 1758 was celebrated with a riot in the narrow street which caused several fatalities.

Called Crow Street in 1756

CUCKOO LANE
off Beresford Street

Perhaps referring to the disreputable habits of cuckoos (the word 'cuckold' derives from 'cuckoo'). Note proximity to Mary's Lane and Mary's Abbey.

Called Cuckoo Lane in 1756

CUFFE STREET
off St Stephen's Green

After Sir James Cuffe who married Alice, daughter of Baron Aungier.

Called Cuffe Street in 1728

See also Aungier Street

THE CUSTOM HOUSE

CUSTOM HOUSE QUAY

After the new Custom House, built amid fierce labour disputes and acrimony in parliament, and opened in 1791. Had a good claim to be

Ireland's finest building until the interior was burned by the IRA in a disastrous action in May 1921.

Called Custom House Quay in 1791

DAME STREET

Dame Gate, the eastern gate of the city, originally stood between Cork Hill and Dame's Lane, now Dame Street. The name is derived from a dam controlling the tide flow at the point where the Poddle joined the Pool of Dublin. The Church of St Mary del Dam acquired its name from the same source. In the fourteenth century Dame Street was also known as the Street of the Thingmote (the mound where Vikings held official ceremonies and assemblies). Widened by the Wide Street Commissioners in 1785–6, the street became an important centre for commerce, banking and insurance. Some unprepossessing sculpture and hideous modern architecture make this street less inviting than it should be.

Called Dame Street in 1610

See also Cork Hill *and* St Andrew's Street

DAWSON STREET
off St Stephen's Green

After Joshua Dawson. He acquired the site in 1705 and built a mansion here in 1710 which was bought for £3,500 in 1715 by Dublin Corporation as the official residence for the Lord Mayor. Now called the Mansion House, it is the venue for many civic functions both social and trade. The first Dáil met here in January 1919.

Number 19 is owned by the Royal Irish Academy, perhaps Ireland's most distinguished centre of learning outside the universities, and holds some ancient manuscripts including the Book of the Dun Cow and the Yellow Book of Lecan. This was once Northland House, built for the Knox family of Tyrone. St Anne's (Church of Ireland) is a fine eighteenth-century building (with a nineteenth-century façade) designed by Isaac Wills. The Royal Hibernian Hotel on the north side, where French officers were imprisoned in comfort in 1798, was demolished in the early 1980s.

Called Dawson Street in 1723

DEAN STREET
off Patrick Street

Originally called Cross Poddle. Renamed by the Wide Street Commissioners, not after Dean Jonathan Swift but from the title of the ecclesiastical head of the nearby St Patrick's Cathedral.

Called Dean Street in 1827

DIGGES STREET
off Mercer Street

Originally Goat Alley in 1728, then Beaux Lane in 1756 which was corrupted to Bow Lane – presumably a favourite promenade for gentlemen. (In 1756 the north side of St Stephen's Green was called Beaux Walk for that reason.) Note proximity to Mercer Street.

C.T. McCready is probably right to conjecture that this was named after a Huguenot settler, a forebear of the Dublin MP Digges La Touche and of West Digges, a Smock Alley actor who quarrelled with Sheridan and provoked a riot in 1754 when Peg Woffington was on stage – a riot which did £9,000 worth of damage and caused Sheridan to leave Dublin.

Called Digges Street in 1735

See also Mercer Street

D'OLIER STREET
joins O'Connell Bridge

After the silversmith Jeremiah D'Olier who, with James Napper Tandy, launched the tempestuous free-trade movement in 1779. He became Sheriff in 1788. Built by the Wide Street Commissioners from 1800. The Steyne or Long Stone, marking the Vikings' first landing spot, stood at the south end. It was still standing in 1669 but was knocked down soon after, presumably being regarded as an obsolete and uninteresting obstruction to traffic. After lying disregarded at the roadside for some time, it simply disappeared – its fate not known.

Called D'Olier Street in 1801

See also Hawkins Street *and* Townsend Street

DOLPHIN'S BARN
joins Cork Street

Probably named after a tavern

Called Dolphin's Barn in 1396

DORSET STREET
joins Bolton Street

After Lionel Cranfield Sackville, 1st Duke of Dorset, Lord Lieutenant 1730–31 and 1750–55.

Richard Brinsley Sheridan was born in number 12 Upper Dorset Street. Sean O'Casey, another distinguished playwright, was born in the house where the Allied Irish Bank now stands.

Called Dorset Street in 1756

See also O'Connell Street

DRURY STREET
meets Exchequer Street

Drury Lane in 1766 and possibly named after the London theatrical street of the same name. Formerly Butter, Boater or Booter Lane Little from the Irish *bóthar* meaning 'road'.

Widened and renamed Drury Street by a consortium of Dublin businessmen which built the impressive South City Markets on the site bounded by Drury Lane, Fade Street, South Great George's Street and Exchequer Street. The markets were rebuilt after a great fire in 1892 and largely demolished in the 1970s.

Called Drury Street in 1886

See also Fade Street *and* Stoneybatter

DUKE STREET
off Grafton Street

After the 2nd Duke of Grafton

Best known for its antique shops and up-market public houses, notably Davy Byrne's (mentioned by James Joyce and frequented by him when he could afford it) and, opposite, the Bailey (a meeting place for Charles Stewart Parnell, the writer Oliver St John Gogarty and Arthur Griffith, founder of Sinn Féin).

Called Duke Street in 1723

See also Grafton Street

EARL STREET, NORTH
off O'Connell Street

After Henry Moore, 1st Earl of Drogheda. He had property north of the River Liffey in the late seventeenth century. The Moores sold out to the Gardiners in 1714 but they must have insisted on the preservation of the family name in several streets such as this one and Moore Street.

Called Earl Street, North in 1756

See also Henry Street, Moore Street *and* O'Connell Street

EARL STREET, SOUTH
off Meath Street

After the Earls of Meath

Called Earl Street, South in 1728

See also Ardee Street

EARLSFORT TERRACE
off St Stephen's Green

After Baron Earlsfort, a title of the 1st Earl of Clonmell.

For long the home of University College Dublin, prior to its move to Belfield. Eoin

MacNeill, founder of the Gaelic League, historian and first Free State Minister for Education taught here as did Thomas MacDonagh, Easter Rising commandant. The acrimonious Treaty debates (December 1921–January 1922) took place here in the university building, originally erected for the Great Exhibition of 1865 and now the National Concert Hall.

Called Earlsfort Terrace in 1839

See also Clonmel Street

ECCLES STREET
off Dorset Street

After Sir John Eccles (owner of Malone Grove near Belfast who prospered after sheltering William of Orange from the rain), Lord Mayor 1710–11, an energetic property developer on the north side. The family sold out to another Ulster family, the Archdalls, in 1748.

The street was immortalised by James Joyce: Molly and Leopold Bloom lived in number 7 (actually the home of Joyce's friend J.F. Byrne). The front door is preserved in the Bailey tavern in Duke Street.

Called Eccles Street in 1772

EDEN QUAY

After William Eden, Baron Auckland, Irish Chief Secretary 1780–82. He failed to marry his daughter to William Pitt the Younger. John Beresford's response to Eden's request: 'I beg that you will contrive to edge my name into some street. . .'

Called Eden Quay in 1796

See also Beresford Place

ELLIS QUAY

After Sir William Ellis, son of a Cambridge don. He eventually became Privy Councillor to James II and served as the exiled king's secretary at St Germain. This quay is the result of the grant of a Dublin Corporation lease of 1682 which stipulated that Sir William build a quay 'for the advantage, ornament and beauty of the city':

Called Ellis Quay in 1766

ELY PLACE

off Baggot Street

After Nicholas Loftus, 1st Earl of Ely, an Ulster magnate. He worked closely with his neighbour Sir Gustavus Hume to develop up-market residential property in the neighbourhood of St Stephen's Green. Hume brought the great architect Cassels to Ireland to build Castle Hume adjacent to Ely Lodge in Fermanagh. Hume married his daughter to the Earl and laid out this street (known for a time as Hume Row).

'Black Jack' Fitzgibbon, 1st Earl of Clare, lived in number 6; after the recall of the popular viceroy, Earl Fitzwilliam, in 1795 a mob surged up the street, Fitzgibbon's sister recalled, 'where, with several smithy sledges, they were working hard to break into his hall door, while some others of them had ropes ready to fix up to his lamp-iron to hang him the moment they could find him'. Disguised as a kitchen maid, Fitzgibbon's sister spread the rumour that the cavalry were approaching and the angry citizens dispersed.

Barry Yelverton, Lord Avonmore, owner of Ballymacarrett in Belfast, lived in number 3; Sir Thornley Stoker in number 8, built in 1770 for the 1st Earl of Ely; the celebrated counsellor and father of Robert Emmet's true love Sarah ('She is far from the land. . .', from Thomas Moore's melody) John Philpot Curran in number 4, later the home of the novelist George Moore; and the writer Oliver St John Gogarty in number 25.

Called Ely Place in 1773

See also Constitution Hill *and* Hume Street

ESSEX QUAY

After Arthur Capel, Earl of Essex, Lord Lieutenant 1672–7.

The designer and maker of medals, William Mossop (1751–1804), lived here.

Called Essex Quay in 1756

See also Capel Street *and* Essex Street, West

ESSEX STREET, WEST
off Fishamble Street

After Essex Quay. This street suffered many changes of name – Stable Alley in 1646, Cadogan's Alley in 1659, Smock Alley in 1661,

Orange Street in 1724 – before acquiring its present name in the nineteenth century. Perhaps it was trying to shake off an unsavoury reputation since, like Petticoat Lane, recorded off St Mary's Abbey in 1756, Smock Alley was a haunt of prostitutes.

A notorious theatre was sited here until 1701 when the gallery collapsed during a performance of Shadwell's *The Libertine*, killing several people. Rebuilt twice again, the theatre survived until 1815. Peg Woffington and Thomas Sheridan acted here.

Called Essex Street, West in 1840

See also Capel Street *and* Essex Quay

EUSTACE STREET
off Dame Street

After Sir Maurice Eustace, Speaker of the Irish House of Commons 1639, Lord Chancellor 1644, whose house and gardens occupied the site.

Called Eustace Street in 1728

EXCHANGE STREET
off Fishamble Street

Recorded as Exchange Alley in 1769. After the Royal Exchange (foundation stone laid 1769, opened 1779) which became the City Hall in September 1852.

Previously called Isod's Lane in 1577 after Isod's or Issolde's Tower on the city wall near Cork Hill. Known as Scarlet Alley in 1619 and Blind Quay n.d.

Called Exchange Street in 1776

See also Cork Hill

EXCHEQUER STREET
off South Great George's Street

After the old site of the medieval Irish Exchequer, where taxes were paid and tallied. In 1728 it is referred to as Chequer Lane and before 1838 it included the present Wicklow Street.

Called Exchequer Street in 1776

FADE STREET
off South Great George's Street

After Joseph Fade, a banker

Called Fade Street in 1756

See also Drury Street

FENIAN STREET
meets Westland Row

After the Fenian Brotherhood, the militant republican movement which organised a rising in 1867 and had strong American connections. Named Denzille Street in 1770 after Ann Denzill of Cornwall, a seventeenth-century ancestor of the 6th Lord Fitzwilliam of Meryon, who laid out this street. Denzille Lane, which runs on to it, preserves the name. Fenian Street now incorporates the former Denzille Street, Harcourt Place and Hamilton Row.

Called Fenian Street in 1924

FISHAMBLE STREET
off Essex Quay

From fish shambles ('shambles' meaning 'slaughterhouse') where fish were gutted and sold. In ancient documents *vicus piscariorum*, 'Fish Street' in 1470 and Fisher Street in 1670. One of the oldest streets. The Celtic church of St Duilech's became St Olaf's in Viking times, Dublin's first parish church. The Northmen had a slipway here, uncovered in the 1970s. Here the Charitable Musical Society built the Musick Hall in 1741, where Handel conducted the first performance of the *Messiah* on 13 April 1742. Henry Grattan, leader of the late-eighteenth-century Patriot Party, and James Clarence Mangan, the poet, were born in this street. In the nineteenth century, the centre of basket-making.

Called Fishamble Street in 1467

FITZWILLIAM STREET
off Merrion Square

After the 6th Lord Fitzwilliam of Meryon who began a large-scale up-market development in the south-east from about 1750 on his own estates – a development which rivalled, and later outstripped, the Gardiner development in the north-east. It is part of what was, until the 1960s, the longest intact Georgian street in Dublin, possibly in the world. Completely straight, ninety-one feet wide, it runs for half a mile from Merrion Square East to Fitzwilliam Place.

The Electricity Supply Board plan in 1961 to

demolish numbers 13–28 provoked an intense controversy in which the Georgian Society lost and the ESB won by demolishing its houses in 1965 and employing Stephenson Gibney Associates to put up replacement offices 1966–70.

Called Fitzwilliam Street in 1792

See also Merrion Square

FLEET STREET
off Westmoreland Street

Probably after the London Fleet Street which derived its name from Old English *fleot* meaning 'flowing water'. Before the building of the quays the waters of the Liffey estuary reached this far at high tide. A much older street than Westmoreland Street which cuts across it, it is now like its London counterpart associated with newspaper production.

Called Fleet Street in 1685

FOLEY STREET
off Amiens Street

After the sculptor John Henry Foley, born in number 6 Montgomery Street. His work includes the O'Connell monument erected in 1854, and the statues of Edmund Burke and Oliver Goldsmith which stand at the front of Trinity College.

Originally Montgomery Street 1776 which gave its name to the notorious 'Monto', Dublin's red-light district, generally left alone by the police until moral pressure became overwhelming in the 1920s. Montgomery was the maiden name of Luke Gardiner's wife.

Called Foley Street *c.* 1930

See also Gardiner Street *and* Waterford Street

FONTENOY STREET
meets Mountjoy Street

After the Belgian village where the Wild Geese, led by Patrick Sarsfield, and with a little help from the French army, routed the combined forces of England, Austria and Holland in 1745, during the War of the Austrian Succession.

Called Fontenoy Street in 1872

See also Sarsfield Quay

FOSTER PLACE
off College Green

After John Foster, Baron Oriel (1740–1828), the last Speaker of the Irish House of Commons and a defiant opponent of Catholic Emancipation and the Union.

Called Foster Place in 1792

See also Burgh Quay *and* Oriel Street

FOWNES STREET
off Dame Street

After Sir William Fownes, Sheriff 1697, Lord Mayor 1708–9. A street of great charm, worthy of the attention of the conservationists presently seeking its preservation.

Called Fownes Street in 1708

See also Cope Street

CHURCH OF ST FRANCIS

FRANCIS STREET
off Thomas Street

After the nearby Church of St Francis, a Franciscan friary founded in 1235 by Ralph de Porter. Catholics worshipped here in Penal times when it was the Catholic Archbishop's chapel. A fair green lay between this street and the south-west walls of the city in medieval times.

Called Francis Street in 1337

FUMBALLY LANE
off New Street

'Fumbally' is a corruption of 'bumbailiff', an officer employed to collect debts and arrest debtors for nonpayment, so called because he followed close behind debtors.

Called Fumbally Lane in 1789

GARDINER STREET

After the second Luke Gardiner (1745–98), celebrated champion of Catholic relief from the Penal Code and MP for Co. Dublin.

Created Viscount Mountjoy in 1795, he was killed leading the Dublin Militia against insurgents during the decisive battle of New Ross in June 1798. The street was laid out by him for the prosperous but its social standing fell rapidly in the nineteenth century. Some improvements were made in the 1940s and 1970s but this long Georgian street is scheduled for redevelopment. Originally the Old Rope Walk 1756, where ropes were made by men walking backwards, twisting the fibres.

For too many Dubliners the street is best known for its Labour Exchange at the south end which was once a Protestant church.

Called Gardiner Street in 1787

See also Foley Street *and* Mountjoy Square

THE CUSTOM HOUSE, FROM GEORGE'S QUAY

GEORGE'S QUAY

After the first Hanoverian, George I (1714–27)

Called George's Quay in 1728

GLOVER'S ALLEY
off Mercer Street

Originally called Rapparee ['Robber'] Alley. Note its proximity to Mercer Street, called Love Lane in 1728 – presumably a red-light district where passers-by were likely to be mugged.

Called Glover's Alley in 1766

GOLDEN LANE
off Bride Street

After the Goldsmiths' Hall which stood here. The original city wall passed through this lane.

Called Golden Lane in 1682

See also Bull Alley

GOLDSMITH STREET
off North Circular Road

After the Irish poet, Oliver Goldsmith (1728–74). His most famous poem, *The Deserted Village,* is thought to be based on Elphin, Co. Roscommon.

Called Goldsmith Street in 1870

GRAFTON STREET
off College Green

After the 2nd Duke of Grafton, Lord Lieutenant at intervals between 1715 and 1723. The most fashionable shopping street in Dublin, and one of the city's first pedestrian precincts. Whyte's Academy was on the site of number 79 and here Richard Brinsley Sheridan, Robert Emmet, Thomas Moore and

PROVOST'S HOUSE, TRINITY COLLEGE

Arthur Wellesley (later the Duke of Wellington) went to school. In 1812 the poet Shelley stayed at number 12.

Called Grafton Street in 1708

See also Duke Street, Henrietta Street *and* Wellington Quay

GRANBY ROW
off Parnell Square

The eldest sons of the Dukes of Rutland bore the title Marquis of Granby. Parnell Square was originally Rutland Square.

Called Granby Row in 1766

See also Parnell Square *and* Rutland Place, West

GREEK STREET
meets Chancery Street

Named in imitation of a neighbouring Latin Court, first recorded in 1756, now defunct. Latin and Greek formed the core curriculum of all schools till the twentieth century. In 1539 the Priory of Friars Preachers was suppressed and the buildings turned into lodgings for lawyers. The Four Courts were later built on the site. The area has a long association with the law (note the nearby Hammond Lane, originally Hangman Lane) and legal documents are still larded with Latin terms. Originally called Cow Lane – perhaps there was pasturage here in early times.

Called Greek Street in 1776

See also Bull Alley *and* Ship Street

GREEN STREET
off King Street, North

Called Abbey Green in 1568 after St Mary's Abbey green. The last public whipping in Dublin took place in 1815 when William Horish was whipped from the gates of the Green Street courthouse to the Royal Exchange in Cork Hill.

Lord Edward Fitzgerald died of his wounds in the cells of the Courthouse in 1798, and it was from the dock in 1803 that Robert Emmet instructed: 'Let no man write my epitaph – when my country takes her place among the nations of the world, then and not till then, let my epitaph be written.'

Called Green Street in 1776

See also Lord Edward Street

HAMMOND LANE
off Church Street

Originally Hangman Lane, first recorded in 1454. The present name is a corruption. A gibbet mede or 'meadow' is recorded nearby in medieval times.

Called Hammond Lane in 1698

HARCOURT STREET
off St Stephen's Green

After the 1st Earl of Harcourt, Lord Lieutenant 1772–6. He drowned in 1777 in an attempt to rescue his dog from a well. Built by John Hatch, Seneschal of the Manor of St Sepulchre and director of the Royal Canal who rented the land from the Earl of Miltown in 1759. Hatch built number 40 for himself where he died in 1797; this building was later the High School until it transferred to Danum estate in Rathgar in the 1960s. Most of the Georgian houses here are either completely rebuilt or due for demolition.

Sir Edward Carson, leader of the Unionist resistance to Home Rule, was born in number 4; number 15 was the mansion of the loathed John Scott, Earl of Clonmell, and it was for a time the Municipal Gallery of Modern Art; Bram Stoker, who gave us *Dracula*, lived in number 16; number 6 was the secret HQ of the Dáil Minister of Finance, Michael Collins, during the Anglo-Irish War (1919–21); and Sir Jonah Barrington MP, supporter of the Union and unmatched raconteur (and forebear of the squash player of the same name) lived at number 14.

Called Harcourt Street in 1775

See also Hatch Street

ST GEORGE'S CHURCH

HARDWICKE PLACE
off Dorset Street

After Philip Yorke, 3rd Earl of Hardwicke, Lord Lieutenant 1801–1806, the first viceroy in office after the Union. St George's Church, built here between 1802 and 1813, is described as 'the finest church in Dublin both as regards situation and design' by Constantia Maxwell in *Dublin Under the Georges*. Number 38½ was Mangan Hall where George Moore and Edward Martyn had their Theatre of Ireland.

Called Hardwicke Street in 1807

HATCH STREET
off Leeson Street

After John Hatch

Called Hatch Street in 1800

See also Harcourt Street

HAWKINS STREET
off Burgh Quay

After Alderman William Hawkins. He

reclaimed tidal mud by building a great wall to channel the River Liffey in 1662. The wall ran close to the Long Stone which traditionally marked the first landing point of the Vikings in the ninth century. The stone gave its name to the district east of Dublin known as the Stein, Staine or Steyne. Between 1862 and 1959 a curious but attractive monument to Surgeon General Sir Philip Crampton stood on the corner of Hawkins Street and College Street.

Called Hawkins Street in 1728

See also D'Olier Street *and* Townsend Street

MOUNTJOY HOUSE

HENRIETTA STREET
off Bolton Street

After Henrietta, wife of Charles, 2nd Duke of Grafton, Lord Lieutenant at intervals between 1715 and 1723. The first important street built by the first Luke Gardiner, it was the most fashionable street in Dublin until after the Union. For many years Dubliners called it 'Primate Hill' because four successive Archbishops of Armagh lived here; Archbishop Stone entertained with 'Polish magnificence', noted Richard Cumberland in his *Memoirs*. Luke Gardiner, his son Viscount Mountjoy, the Earl of Kingston, the Earl of Thomand, and Gardiner's grandson, the Earl of Blessington lived here.

The King's Inns of Court dominate the west end; built between 1795 and 1817, to the design of James Gandon, this building houses the ruling body of the Irish legal profession.

Called Henrietta Street in 1724

See also Grafton Street

HENRY STREET
off O'Connell Street

After Henry Moore, 1st Earl of Drogheda. A favourite shopping street, brilliantly illuminated at Christmas. The scene of fierce fighting at the close of the Easter Rising 1916.

Called Henry Street in 1724

See also Earl Street, North

HIGH STREET
joins Christchurch Place

After its height and importance in ancient times when it was the principal thoroughfare. Recorded as the *altus vicus*, 'High Street', in Anglo-Norman times and Main Street in 1240. There was a High Cross where High Street, St Nicholas Street, Christchurch Place and St Michael's Hill now meet. Some of the finest remains of the Viking world were found here in the 1960s and excavated in the 1970s. St Audeon's (originally St Colmcille's, a Viking parish church) is a much-restored Norman church of great character where part of the old city wall can be seen.

Called High Street in 1307

HILL STREET
joins Parnell Street

So called because of its location on a hill. Originally the lower part of Temple Street, first recorded in 1800, and renamed by the Dublin Corporation because of its bad reputation. At first they had threatened to change it to Chatterton Street, to dishonour the name of the Rt. Hon. Hedges Eyre Chatterton, Vice chancellor, who had opposed changing the name of Sackville Street to O'Connell Street.

Called Hill Street in 1886

See also Temple Street, North

HOLLES STREET
off Merrion Square

After the family name of Eleanor the wife of Oliver, 2nd Viscount Fitzwilliam of Meryon, forebear of the 6th Viscount who laid out this and neighbouring streets.

Called Holles Street in 1773

See also Clare Street *and* Merrion Square

HUME STREET
off St Stephen's Green

After Mary Hume, daughter of the Fermanagh

landlord/surgeon/urban building speculator Sir Gustavus Hume, who married Nicholas Loftus, 1st Earl of Ely.

This street, for long occupied by the well-to-do, leaped to prominence in December 1969 when students of architecture occupied number 45 in an attempt to prevent property developers tearing down this and other houses next to it. The students, who received impressive support, succeeded only in forcing the developers to give their replacement buildings a neo-Georgian façade.

Called Hume Street in 1768

See also Ely Place

INNS QUAY

After the King's Inns of Court, which took over the dissolved Dominican friary here from 1541 until 1775 when the site was cleared to make way for the Public Record Office designed by Thomas Cooley. The Record Office was destroyed by a huge land mine laid by the Irregulars at the conclusion of the siege of the Four Courts in April–June 1922 which began the Irish Civil War. Documents going back to the twelfth century floated all over Dublin, prompting Churchill's comment: 'Better a state without archives than archives without a state.'

The Four Courts, built to James Gandon's design between 1786 and 1802, is one of Dublin's most splendid buildings. It still bears the marks of the siege: following artillery bombardment by the National Army, the

Irregulars set fire to the building which destroyed Gandon's interior and melted the copper dome (now replaced).

Called Inns Quay in 1743
See also Chancery Place

DANIEL O'CONNELL CENTENARY CELEBRATION IN DUBLIN
—THE PROCESSION PASSING THE FOUR COURTS

ISLAND STREET
off Bridgefoot Street

After Usher's Island. Originally Dunghill Lane.

Called Island Street in 1756

See also Usher's Island

JAMES'S STREET
joins Thomas Street

After the ancient St James's Church which existed in 1584. The start of a public whipping course in the eighteenth century: for example, the thief William Grace was condemned 'to be whipt from the Tholsel of St James Street on Wednesday next'. Once well known for its Foundling Hospital the street is famous today as the home of the Guinness brewery, at one time the largest in the world. It was here, according to the song, the 'Twangman' murdered his rival in love:

> He lay in wait, by James's Gate
> Till the poor oul' Bags came up
> And with his twang knife he took the life
> Of the poor oul' gather-him-up.

Called James's Street in 1610

JERVIS STREET
off Parnell Street

After shipowner Sir Humphrey Jervis, Sheriff 1674, Lord Mayor 1681. He was rewarded with land in this area from the estate of St Mary's Abbey for his services in building Essex Bridge in 1676 with stone he obtained by almost demolishing the abbey.

Called Jervis Street in 1728

See also Abbey Street, Ormond Quay *and* Swift's Alley

JOHN'S LANE WEST

off Thomas Street

After St John's Church near Cornmarket mentioned in 1177. Formerly called Tenniscourt Lane, first recorded in 1610. Presumably a precursor of Wimbledon. In Penal times the Augustinian Father Byrne converted an old stable here into a chapel.

Called John's Lane West in 1756

KEVIN STREET

runs from Patrick Street to Wexford Street

An ancient thoroughfare taking its name from St Kevin's Church mentioned in 1317, which also gave its name to the medieval gate situated in Wexford Street. The link between Kevin Street Upper and Kevin Street Lower was once named St Kevin's Cross Street.

Called Kevin Street in 1577

KILDARE STREET

off St Stephen's Green

After James Fitzgerald, 20th Earl of Kildare, then Viscount Leinster, then Earl of Offaly and Marquis of Kildare, and finally 1st Duke of Leinster 1761–6. His town house, Leinster House, is now the home of the Irish legislature, purchased from the Royal Dublin Society, now in Ballsbridge.

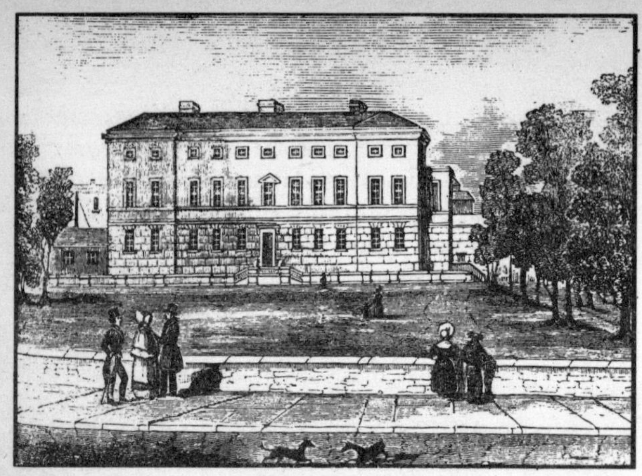

LEINSTER HOUSE

Originally Coote Lane, after the Cootes of Cootehill who married into the Molesworth family. Bought from Lord Molesworth by the 20th Earl of Kildare in 1744, and widened and renamed by him. The National Library and the National Museum flank Leinster House in matching buildings.

Called Kildare Street in 1756

See also Leinster Street *and* Lord Edward Street

KING STREET, NORTH
joins Bolton Street

Either after Henry VIII, ratified by the Irish Parliament as King of Ireland in 1541, or after the boy king Edward VI (1547–53) in gratitude for a Protestant succession.

Called King Street, North in 1552

KING STREET, SOUTH
off St Stephen's Green

Either named to celebrate the accession of

George II in 1727 or after William King, Archbishop of Dublin 1703–29, an energetic church and school builder and an even more energetic persecutor of Catholics and Presbyterians. Scene of fighting at the end of the Easter Rising 1916 and alleged murders by the South Staffordshire Regiment.

Called King Street, South in 1728

KING'S INNS STREET
off Bolton Street

After the neighbouring King's Inns of Court opened in Henrietta Street in 1809. Originally called Turnagain Lane.

Called King's Inns Street *c.* 1800

LEESON STREET
off St Stephen's Green

After Joseph Leeson, created Earl of Miltown in 1735. With the Fitzwilliams and Dawsons, he did much to make the south-east of the city a fashionable quarter. Leeson Street lies on the ancient road south to Donnybrook. In the 1870s Sir Arthur Edward Guinness, Baron Ardilaun, built a lavish mansion here used during the Second World War as an air-raid precautions store. Gutted by fire in 1943, it was pulled down in 1968. Early in the twentieth century the novelist George Moore complained that this elegant street had 'fallen into the hands of nuns and lodging housekeepers'.

Called Leeson Street in 1756

LEINSTER STREET
joins Nassau Street

After James Fitzgerald, 1st Duke of Leinster

Called Leinster Street in 1756

See also Kildare Street

CHAPTER PLACE, SHOWING A CORNER OF ST PATRICK'S

THE LIBERTIES

Residential areas beyond the city walls, so named because those living there were free from certain taxes and obligations imposed within the city. The Liberties were of: St Patrick (around the cathedral); St Sepulchre (surrounding Francis Street); St Thomas (around St Mary's Abbey, renamed Liberty of the Earl of Meath in the sixteenth century); St

Mary (on the north side of the River Liffey).

To most Dubliners today, the Liberties designate the area around St Patrick's Cathedral, The Coombe and Thomas Street. The notable rise in local pride is celebrated in the writings and broadcasts of Eamonn Mac Thomáis and Elgy Gillespie.

Called the Liberties in the fourteenth century

See also Meath Street

LIFFEY STREET
off Bachelor's Walk

After the River Liffey. The old name for the river was Ruirthech, meaning 'violent stream'. Liffey, or Life, referred to the plain to the west of Dublin. For long it was called Anna Liffey from *abhainn life*, meaning 'river [of the plain of] Liffey'.

Called Liffey Street in 1728

LINCOLN PLACE
joins Leinster Street

After President Lincoln of America. Unlike the British government of the day, the Dublin Corporation knew which side it sympathised with in the American Civil War. The reason for the name change was more prosaic: this street (known as St Patrick's Lane in 1756, Park Place in 1773 and Park Street in 1792) had an unsavoury reputation as the resort of prostitutes, no doubt patronised by Trinity students emerging from the university's back gate.

Called Lincoln Place in 1862

LINENHALL STREET
off King Street, North

After the adjacent Linen Hall, opened in 1726, which was the principal market place for Irish linen cloth, particularly for overseas buyers. It was demolished after the First World War. Surrounding streets were named after the Ulster towns which marketed their linen here until a dispute with the Linen Board in the 1780s. There was also a Yarn Hall nearby.

Called Linenhall Street in 1756

See also Coleraine Street, Lisburn Street, Lurgan Street *and* Yarnhall Street

LISBURN STREET
off Coleraine Street

After the Ulster linen town

Called Lisburn Street in 1756

See also Linenhall Street

LORD EDWARD STREET
joins Cork Hill

After Lord Edward Fitzgerald, son of James Fitzgerald, 1st Duke of Leinster. Fought for the British in the American War of Independence 1781; admitted to the Bear tribe of Indians; radical MP; married Pamela, daughter of Philippe Egalité, Duke of Orleans; a leader of the revolutionary United Irishmen in 1798 but arrested and mortally wounded on the eve of the rising. The street was built by the Dublin Corporation to relieve congestion of traffic past Dublin Castle. The street probably runs, through the site of the Vikings' 'Longport' or stockade for protecting their vessels.

Called Lord Edward Street in 1886

See also Green Street, Kildare Street, Thomas Street *and* Werburgh Street

LOTTS
off Liffey Street

After the area known as the 'Lots' when, in 1717–18, Dublin Corporation drew lots for possession of the land to be reclaimed by the building of the North Wall completed in 1729.

Called Lotts in 1756

See also North Wall

LOVE LANE
off Mount Street, Lower

Presumably once a red-light area

Called Love Lane in 1824

LOWER ABBEY STREET *see* Abbey Street

LOWER MOUNT STREET *see* Mount Street, Lower

LUKE STREET
off Townsend Street

After St Luke. Perhaps refers to the nearby St Mark's Church since the two apostles are frequently associated. The Lock Hospital, later the Hospital of St Margaret of Cortona, stood here at the corner of Townsend Street until it was demolished in the 1950s.

Called Luke Street in 1756

See also Mark's Alley

LURGAN STREET
off King Street, North

After the Ulster linen town

Called Lurgan Street in 1756

See also Linenhall Street

MARK STREET
off Townsend Street

After the neighbouring St Mark's Church, built in 1729.

Called Mark Street in 1773

MARK'S ALLEY
off Francis Street

After St Mark. Perhaps refers to the nearby St Luke's Church since the two apostles are frequently associated.

Called Mark's Alley in 1728

See also Luke Street

MARLBOROUGH STREET
off Eden Quay

After John Churchill, 1st Duke of Marlborough (1650–1722), ancestor of Sir Winston Churchill. Developed by the Beresford family which acquired some of the lands of St Mary's Abbey in 1717. Sir Marcus Beresford, Earl of Tyrone, married into the Piphoe family which also had property here. The great granite mansion, Tyrone House, was designed by Richard Cassels and built from 1740; it is now the home of the Department of Education. The Pro-Cathedral, based on plans by Louis Le Bas sent from Paris by the United

TYRONE HOUSE

Irishman John Sweetman, was begun in 1816.

Called Marlborough Street in 1728

See also Beresford Place, Eden Quay, Phibsborough Road *and* Waterford Street

MARROWBONE LANE
off Cork Street

Possibly a corruption of St Mary le Bone

Called Marrowbone Lane in 1743

See also Tenterfields

MARSHALSEA LANE
off Thomas Street

After the Marshalsea, or debtors' prison, moved here from a site near Wood Quay at the turn of the century. Conditions for the inmates were vile, only the very poorest being given free bread. Later used as a barracks and, until 1970, as a temporary home for Dublin Corporation tenants. Demolished in 1975.

Called Marshalsea Lane in 1825

MARY STREET
off Capel Street

After St Mary's Abbey. James Joyce opened the Volta Cinema (later the Lyceum) here in 1909, but the venture was not a success. Number 29 was used secretly as an office by Michael Collins during the Anglo-Irish War. The decayed Church of Ireland church was built at Archbishop William King's behest in 1700; Wolfe Tone (the United Irishmen leader), James Caulfield, 1st Earl of Charlemont (Patriot leader), and Sean O'Casey (dramatist) were baptised here; John Wesley gave his first sermon in Ireland here; and Archibald Hamilton Rowan (the United Irishman who evaded arrest by rowing to France in an open boat) is buried in the churchyard.

Called Mary Street in 1728

See also Abbey Street

MARY'S ABBEY
off Capel Street

After St Mary's Abbey. Called Mary's Lane in 1438. A Petticoat Lane is recorded in 1756 off Mary's Lane, and Coney Street off Petticoat Lane in 1766. 'Coney', or 'rabbit', was a common term for a 'mark' or victim used by cardsharps and con men, so presumably, in the eighteenth century at least, this was a disreputable area.

Called Mary's Abbey in 1215

See also Abbey Street *and* Mary's Lane

MARY'S LANE
joins Greek Street

After St Mary's Abbey. This is not to be confused with the Mary's Lane recorded in 1438 which referred to the street now named Mary's Abbey.

Called Mary's Lane in 1610

See also Mary's Abbey

MEATH STREET
off The Coombe

After the Earls of Meath. The heart of the Liberties, closely watched by the military in 1798 and giving support to Robert Emmet in 1803. The Meath Hospital was completed here in 1773 to minister to the poor of the Earl of Meath's Liberty but the institution moved to new premises behind Kevin Street in Long Lane in 1822.

Called Meath Street in 1728

See also Ardee Street *and* the Liberties

MERCER STREET
off York Street

After Mary Mercer who endowed a hospital for the sick poor, opened in 1734 on or near the site of an ancient leper hospital. Called Love Lane in 1728, Little Cuffe Street in 1733, French Street in 1776 and, in a final attempt to shake off an unsavoury reputation, Mercer Street in 1860.

Called Mercer Street in 1860

See also Digges Street

MERCHANTS' QUAY

Second only to Wood Quay as the oldest quay in Dublin. Originally it extended from the Crane at the bottom of Winetavern Street to the Old Bridge (now Father Matthew Bridge).

Until the mid-eighteenth century it was a principal residence of merchants – hence its name. Among the gentry who lived here in the seventeenth century were Sir Philip Perceval, Sir William Parsons, and the Jacobite Lord Mayor, Sir Thomas Hackett. It was for a long time narrow and congested (which is why Robert Emmet planned to attack the military here with a rocket battery at the Crane in 1803) until cleared by the Wide Street Commissioners from about 1816 onwards.

Called Merchants' Quay *c.* fourteenth century

ANTRIM HOUSE

MERRION SQUARE

After the 6th Lord Fitzwilliam of Meryon who developed his low-lying estate bounded today by Leeson Street in the west and St Patrick's Well Lane, Denzille Lane and Grand Canal Street. Planned by John Ensor, it is probably Dublin's finest Georgian square. Antrim House, built by Ensor, was demolished in the 1930s. In recent years the general public has had access to the railed-in park.

Called Merrion Square in 1762

See also Fitzwilliam Street *and* Holles Street

MESPIL ROAD
off Leeson Street, Upper

After a country house built close to Leeson Street Bridge in 1751 by a Dr Barry. Mespil House, last owned by the artist Sarah Purser, is now demolished and replaced by blocks of flats. The Irish Life Building, completed 1962, has a good claim to be the most pleasing example of modern Dublin architecture. Gallows Hill and Gibbet Meadow are recorded near here in the mid-sixteenth century.

Called Mespil Road in 1821

See also Mount Street, Lower

MICHAEL'S HILL
off High Street

After the nearby St Michael's Church, mentioned in 1178, rebuilt in 1812 and demolished in 1872 when the Synod Hall was erected on the site. Originally named Gillamocholmog's Street in 1218 after the tribal chiefs who included the King of Leinster in 1103 and the main ruler of Dublin 1125–34. Then called Michael's Lane, it took over the name of Michael's Hill from the street alongside Christ Church Cathedral (originally Christchurch Lane) after it was incorporated into Winetavern Street. The houses here were demolished in 1964.

Called Michael's Hill in the thirteenth century

MIDDLE ABBEY STREET *see* Abbey Street

HOUSE OF THE SPEAKER
OF THE IRISH HOUSE OF COMMONS

MOLESWORTH STREET
off Dawson Street

After the Molesworth family. Robert, 1st Viscount Molesworth (1656–1725), was a Fishamble Street merchant who made his fortune supplying tents to Cromwell and bought land here known as 'Molesworth Fields'. The street was laid out by Richard, 3rd Viscount Molesworth. Still an exclusive street, it has lost most of its fine Georgian houses nevertheless.

Called Molesworth Street in 1727

MOLYNEUX YARD
off Thomas Street

After the Molyneux family. Sir Thomas Molyneux (1531–97) was Chancellor of the Exchequer in Ireland in 1590. His son Daniel was Ulster King of Arms. Daniel's son Samuel built a mansion in New Row where his sons William (1656–98) and Thomas (1661–1733) were born. William was a philosopher, politician and author of *The case of Ireland's being bound by Acts of Parliament in England stated. . .* Thomas was a physician and

Professor of Medicine in Dublin. Several of his papers on zoological subjects broke new ground. He built Molyneaux House in Peter Street, which was later taken over by showman Philip Astley, who built an amphitheatre behind it where he presented equestrian spectaculars.

Called Molyneux Yard in 1756

MOORE STREET
off Henry Street

After Henry Moore, 1st Earl of Drogheda. Celebrated as a vegetable market and for its loquacious street sellers. Scene of the last offensive by the GPO insurgents in the Easter Rising 1916.

Called Moore Street in 1728

See also Earl Street, North

MOUNT BROWN *see* Cromwell's Quarters

MOUNT STREET, LOWER
off Merrion Square

Charles Haliday suggests that the name derived from the 'rocky gallows mount' between Lower Baggot Street (Gallows Row in 1756) and Lower Mount Street.

J.M. Synge, playwright, died here at number 130 in 1909. On Wednesday 26 April 1916 a dozen insurgents held up several companies of Sherwood Foresters. Shooting mainly from Clanwilliam House (now demolished) at the southern end, the men under De Valera's command inflicted 234 casualties – half those incurred by British forces throughout the Easter Rising.

Called Mount Street, Lower in 1790

See also Mespil Road

MOUNTJOY SQUARE

After Viscount Mountjoy. A four-acre plot once surrounded by seventy-two houses. Never a commercial success, the square rapidly slid down the social scale. By the time preservationists sought to reverse the decline, it was too late. The Dublin Corporation (which took over most of the houses in 1938) vacillated between demolition and restoration in the 1960s and 1970s and ended up by doing a bit of both.

Called Mountjoy Square in 1792

See also Blessington Street *and* Gardiner Street

NASSAU STREET
meets Grafton Street

Possibly after William III but more likely after Count Henry Nassau who led in the Dutch Blue Guards to 'liberate' Dublin from the Jacobites after the Williamite victory at the Boyne on 1 July 1690. Now a fashionable shopping street facing the south side of Trinity College, much favoured by tourists.

Called Nassau Street in 1756

See also St Andrew's Street

NEW STREET
joins Patrick Street

In fact one of the oldest streets of what was

once suburban Dublin. It seemed new at the time.

Called New Street in 1218

NICHOLAS STREET
off High Street

After the nearby Church of St Nicholas, built by Bishop Donagh, first Bishop of Dublin in 1038. It was rebuilt in 1578 and 1707 before being finally demolished about 1840.

Called Nicholas Street in 1190

NORTH BRUNSWICK STREET *see* Brunswick Street, North

NORTH CIRCULAR ROAD

Part of a thoroughfare encircling central Dublin. The northern section is three miles long, extending from the North Wall to Phoenix Park. The Royal Canal was planned to run parallel. A favourite road for the fashionable to drive along as Lord Cloncurry remembered in 1849:

> Upon that magnificent drive I have frequently seen three or four coaches and six, and eight or ten coaches and four, passing slowly to and fro in a long procession of other carriages and between a double column of well-mounted horsemen.

Called North Circular Road in 1763

NORTH EARL STREET *see* Earl Street, North

NORTH GREAT GEORGE'S STREET
off Parnell Street

After George III (1760–1820). Isaac Butt,

founder of the Home Rule movement, bought number 41 in 1876. John Dillon, who helped Parnell to oust Butt and then ousted Parnell in 1891 to lead the Anti-Parnellites and become the last leader of the Irish Parliamentary Party only to be ousted himself by Sinn Féin in 1918, lived in number 2. The poet and antiquary Sir Samuel Fergusson (1810–86) lived in number 20 and the cantankerous Trinity Provost, John Pentland Mahaffy, opponent of Douglas Hyde and founder of the Irish Georgian Society, owned number 38. Once one of the finest Georgian streets, it is currently becoming fashionable again, thanks to the efforts of Senator David Norris.

Called North Great George's Street in 1776

NORTH KING STREET *see* King Street, North

NORTH TEMPLE STREET *see* Temple Street, North

NORTH WALL

After its location on the north side of the river. It was here that a ship arrived every week from Liverpool bringing food for the locked-out workers in Dublin in 1913, and paid for by British trade unionists.

Called North Wall in 1729

See also Lotts

O'CONNELL STREET

After Daniel O'Connell (1775–1847) who won emancipation for Catholics in 1829.

First laid out as Drogheda Street by the Moore family but renamed Sackville Street after

O'CONNELL STREET

Lionel Cranfield Sackville, 1st Duke of Dorset, Lord Lieutenant 1730–31 and 1750–55 when rebuilt by the first Luke Gardiner in the 1740s. Gardiner intended the forty-eight-foot wide street as an exclusive residential area with a large enclosed mall or promenade. The street was opened up by the Wide Street Commissioners who built Lower Sackville Street in 1784, erected Carlisle (now O'Connell) Bridge in 1790 and created D'Olier and Westmoreland Streets from 1800. When Carlisle Bridge was widened in 1880 the street had already become Dublin's main thoroughfare. It provided as dramatic a vista as could be found in any European capital, a scene which could be enjoyed from the top of Nelson Pillar (designed by Francis Johnston and completed in 1829).

The labour leader James Larkin, wearing a false beard and Count Markievicz's frock coat, addressed a meeting of locked-out workers from the balcony of the Imperial (now Gresham) Hotel in 1913, precipitating a notorious police charge which was a prologue of greater violence to come.

THE NELSON PILLAR

All was changed, changed utterly by the Easter Rising in 1916. About three-quarters of the street was destroyed by shells fired from Trinity College and the gunboat *Helga*. Further destruction followed in 1922 when Irregulars occupied part of the street; in defeating them the National Army destroyed the Granville and Hamman Hotels, the YMCA and the premises of the Hibernian Society.

The Nelson Pillar was blown up, probably by the IRA, on the night of 7 March 1966 and the remaining stump was removed soon afterwards.

Bustling with fast-food bars, souvenir shops and business premises, the street is dominated by the surviving portico of Francis Johnston's General Post Office (built in 1818 and the HQ of the Easter Rising insurgents) and the monuments to the Home Rule leader Parnell at the north end and to O'Connell at the south. The trees down the centre provided a unique winter habitat for a population of long-tailed tits, until ousted by traffic fumes in the 1970s. A vigorous programme of commercial development is presently sweeping aside the seedy appearance much of the street had acquired by the early 1980s.

Dublin Corporation voted to change the name of Sackville Street to O'Connell Street in December 1884 but the alteration was prevented by a court injuncion, produced the following year at the behest of the residents. It was not until May 1924 that the name change became official.

Called O'Connell Street in 1924

See also Dorset Street *and* Earl Street, North

OLIVER BOND STREET
meets Bridgefoot Street

After Oliver Bond, the Bridge Street woollen merchant arrested with his fellow United Irish conspirators in 1798. Though a modern street, it follows the line of the medieval Crockers Street, named from the potters who lived and worked there. The western end is remembered in a cul-de-sac off Marshalsea Lane called Croker Lane.

Called Oliver Bond Street in 1936

See also Bridge Street *and* Croker Lane

ORIEL STREET
off Sheriff Street

After John Foster, Baron Oriel (1740–1828), the last Speaker of the Irish House of Commons. Perhaps also inspired by the adjacent Commons Street.

Called Oriel Street in 1832

See also Burgh Quay *and* Foster Place

ORMOND QUAY

After James Butler, 1st Duke of Ormonde, Lord Lieutenant 1643–9 and 1660–69.

Ormond Quay Upper, recorded in 1742, covers the 'pill' or small river inlet that branched off from the Liffey before the river was held back by the quay walls.

Built by Sir Humphrey Jervis, a shipowner who later became Sheriff in 1674 and Lord Mayor in 1681 and who bought twenty acres of the lands of St Mary's Abbey in 1674. Jervis intended to build houses right up to the water's edge but Ormonde persuaded him to build a quay – a pattern thereafter followed on both sides of the River Liffey. Cattle drivers and butchers from the quay frequently fought Protestant weavers from The Coombe in the eighteenth century, using the Liffey bridges as a battleground.

Called Ormond Quay in 1678

See also Jervis Street *and* Ormond Street

ORMOND STREET
off Cork Street

After James Butler, 1st Duke of Ormonde

Called Ormond Street in 1756

See also Ormond Quay

PARLIAMENT STREET
off Dame Street

After the Irish Parliament which voted the money for its building by the Wide Street Commissioners to connect Dublin Castle with

Capel Street via Essex Bridge. Until the opening up of Sackville Street and the construction of Carlisle Bridge in 1790, this was part of the main route to the north of the city. A Silk Warehouse was erected here in 1765 as a sales hall for the Dublin Spitalfields weavers but it fell into disuse following the demise of the industry in the early nineteenth century.

Called Parliament Street in 1760

See also Spitalfields

CHARLEMONT HOUSE

PARNELL SQUARE

After Charles Stewart Parnell, the leader of the Irish Parliamentary Party 1879–91. Formerly Rutland Square, 1753–69, after Charles Manners, 4th Duke of Rutland, Lord Lieutenant 1784–7. Development began in 1748 when Dr Bartholomew Mosse leased land at the top of Sackville Street to build the Rotunda Hospital. Soon after, the first Luke Gardiner began the building of the east side of the square (he named the lower part of this road Cavendish Row and the name plate is still in place). Thereafter Mosse and Gardiner co-operated to complete the square. By the

1780s Rutland Square was the most exclusive in Dublin: twelve MPs, eleven peers, two bishops and one peeress lived there in 1792. On the north side, formerly Palace Row, James Caulfield, 1st Earl of Charlemont, built his town house which is now the Municipal Gallery of Modern Art, intermittently housing the collection of Sir Hugh Lane, drowned in the *Lusitania* in 1915.

Called Parnell Square in 1933

See also Charlemont Street, Granby Row, Parnell Street *and* Rutland Place, West

THE LYING-IN HOSPITAL AND ROTUNDA

PARNELL STREET

Originally Great Britain Street in 1728. Noted particularly for the Lying-in Hospital, better known as the Rotunda, and probably the first maternity hospital in the British Isles. The Rotunda, begun in 1764 and given further decoration in 1786, served as a function room for raising money for the hospital. Here the pianist and composer John Field gave the first public performance of his music (he invented the nocturne); the Volunteers met in 1783 to demand parliamentary reform; and Eoin MacNeill founded the Irish Volunteers in 1913. The Rotunda is also the home of one of the liveliest of Dublin's theatres, the Gate. The gardens behind the hospital started out as an eighteenth-century leisure centre for fund raising but were built over piecemeal. The remaining land has been made into a Garden of Remembrance for those who died 1916–22 in the struggle for independence.

Called Parnell Street in 1911

See also Parnell Square

ST PATRICK'S CATHEDRAL

PATRICK STREET

After St Patrick's Church, promoted to Cathedral in 1213. A street which ran parallel to the Poddle, extending from St Patrick's Cathedral to the old city walls. The poverty of the people here influenced Dean Swift in his many writings, particularly *Drapier's Letters*. In 1891 the travel writer Madame de Bovet described it a street 'consisting of two rows of tumble-down mouldy-looking houses, reeking of dirt and oozing with the disgusting smell of accumulated filth of many generations. . .' She noticed that 'every other shop is an old clothes shop'. In the song, 'Biddy Mulligan' says:

> By Patrick Street corner for thirty-five years
> I stood by me stall, that's no lie. . .

And in the second verse:

> Of a Saturday night I sell second-hand clothes,
> From me stall on the floor of the street. . .

Called Patrick Street in 1285

PEARSE STREET

After Patrick Pearse (1879–1916), schoolmaster, writer, Irish language enthusiast and republican insurgent executed in 1916. He was brought up in number 27.

Originally Great Brunswick Street, 1795, after the Hanoverian family connection.

Named Pearse Street in 1923

PHIBSBOROUGH ROAD
meets North Circular Road

After the Piphoe family which held land in north Dublin from medieval times to the eighteenth century.

Called Phibsborough Road in 1792

See also Marlborough Street

PHOENIX STREET
off Arran Street, West

After the nearby park which derives its name

AQUEDUCT, PHIBSBOROUGH

from the spring well near the Phoenix Pillar. In Irish the spring was called *fionn uisce* meaning 'clear water' which was corrupted by English speakers to 'feen ix'. Philip Stanhope, the 4th Earl of Chesterfield, who erected the pillar in 1745, had it surmounted by a phoenix rising from its ashes which has led to the popular misconception that the park is called after the fabled bird.

Called Phoenix Street in 1756

LIGHTHOUSE, SOUTH WALL

PIGEONHOUSE ROAD

After the Pigeon House which was first a storage place for shipwrecked goods, then a hotel for those crossing the Irish Sea, then a fort or an explosives store, then a military dock. In 1814 the government paid the Harbour Board

£100,183 for the basin and buildings. It was probably called after a John Pigeon who was employed there in 1786. It has been variously named South Wall in 1766, Lighthouse Wall – after Poolbeg Lighthouse, completed in 1767 – and Ballast Office Wall.

Called Pigeonhouse Road in 1786

POOLBEG STREET
off Hawkins Street

So called because it leads to the Poolbeg or 'little pool', one of the two deep-water pools in the harbour, the other being the larger pool of Clontarf.

Called Poolbeg Street in 1728

RAILWAY STREET
off Gardiner Street

So called because of its proximity to the Amiens Street railway terminus, Connolly Station.

Called Railway Street in 1911

See also Waterford Street

RICHMOND PLACE
joins North Circular Road

After Charles Lennox, 4th Duke of Richmond, Lord Lieutenant 1807–13. This peer was particularly eager to have streets and buildings named after him, for example Richmond Street North and Richmond Street South.

Called Richmond Place in 1818

RUTLAND PLACE, WEST
off Parnell Square

After Charles Manners, 4th Duke of Rutland, Lord Lieutenant 1784–7.

Called Rutland Place, West *c.* 1780s

See also Granby Row *and* Parnell Square

ST ANDREW'S STREET
off Suffolk Street

After St Andrew's Church, built in 1670, burned down in 1860 and rebuilt in 1866. It stands on or near the site of an ancient church called the Church of St Andrew de Thengmote. The Thingmote was a massive mound built by the Vikings as a place for law-making and debate (as in Thing, Althing, Thingwall, Dingwall and Tynwald). It was levelled in the seventeenth century, the surplus soil being used to raise the level of St Patrick's Well Lane (now Nassau Street).

Called St Andrew's Street 1776

See also Dame Street, Nassau Street *and* Suffolk Street

ST MICHAN'S STREET
off Chancery Street

After St Michan's Church. In medieval times it was called Fishers Lane.

Called St Michan's Street in 1890

See also Church Street

ST STEPHEN'S GREEN

After St Stephen's Church, 1224–1639,

ST STEPHEN'S GREEN

originally attached to a leper hospital on or near the site of Mercer's Hospital. The Green was a grazing common outside the city until 1664 when the bankrupt Dublin Corporation enclosed twenty-seven acres behind a stone wall and laid out building plots in another thirty acres surrounding the square. At first those who lived here were drawn from a wide range of social classes; some of the neighbouring streets such as Digges Street and Glover's Alley had an unsavoury reputation and it may be significant that the north side of the Green was called Beaux Walk in the eighteenth century.

By the late eighteenth century this earliest and largest of Dublin's squares had become a very fashionable quarter. Great men had their town houses here. Thomas Fitzmaurice, the Earl of Kerry (whose son, the Marquis of Shelburne, became a British Prime Minister) built Kerry House on the north side; sold as a barracks in 1795, it held prisoners in 1798. Accidentally burned down, it was replaced by the Shelbourne Hotel. The two finest mansions are both on the south side: Iveagh House (built

ROYAL COLLEGE OF SURGEONS

1730), now the Department of External Affairs, and Newman House (completed 1765) once the Catholic University where the poet Gerard Manley Hopkins was a professor.

The gardens of the Green, landscaped by the Guinness family, were seized by insurgents under Countess Markievicz's command in 1916 and fierce fighting followed in the Royal College of Surgeons (built 1806) on the west side. St Stephen's Green is always bursting with life, its shops thronged and the ducks and seagulls well fed on fine days.

Called St Stephen's Green in 1250

SARSFIELD QUAY

After Patrick Sarsfield, the Irish commander of the Wild Geese. Originally Pembroke Quay in 1756, after Thomas Herbert, 8th Earl of Pembroke, Lord Lieutenant 1707–9.

Called Sarsfield Quay in 1887

See also Fontenoy Street

SCHOOLHOUSE LANE
off Kildare Street

After St Anne's Schoolhouse, built in 1757

Called Schoolhouse Lane in 1757

EIGHTEENTH-CENTURY HOUSES

SEAN MAC DERMOTT STREET
off O'Connell Street

After the Co. Leitrim patriot and Irish Republican Brotherhood leader who organised and fought in the 1916 Easter Rising. Executed after the insurrection.

Originally Gloucester Street, first recorded in 1776, after William Henry, Duke of Gloucester and Edinburgh, brother of George III. Laid out in 1772 with many large houses, the street became dilapidated and overcrowded in the late-nineteenth and twentieth centuries. After St Thomas's Church was destroyed in the Civil War, the street was extended to run directly into O'Connell Street. Most of the tenements are cleared now and replaced with Dublin Corporation flats.

Called Sean Mac Dermott Street in 1933

SHIP STREET
off Stephen's Street

After 'sheep', not a vessel. This was the entrance to grazing land referred to in 1411 as 'le Shepe's land'. By the eighteenth century, however, the name had become corrupted to Ship Street.

Called Ship Street in 1728

See also Bull Alley *and* Greek Street

SIR JOHN ROGERSON'S QUAY

After the alderman who became Chief Justice of the King's Bench. The quay was built as part of an ambitious project undertaken by the Ballast Office to make the River Liffey estuary more navigable. Rogerson leased some of the land reclaimed by this scheme.

Called Sir John Rogerson's Quay in 1728

SKIPPERS' ALLEY
off Merchants' Quay

After sea captains who moored their vessels at Merchants' Quay and took lodgings during their stay. By the end of the seventeenth century skippers could not have come so far upriver.

Earlier known as Lowestock Lane.

Called Skippers' Alley in 1605

SMITHFIELD
off King Street, North

Probably a conscious imitation of the London cattle market, it was created when Oxmantown Green was divided up for building development, with the specific reservation of some land for a road and a market.

Called Smithfield in 1697

See also Blackhall Place

SOUTH CIRCULAR ROAD

So named because it encircled the city south of the River Liffey. Part of an ambitious project of town planning undertaken by the Wide Street Commissioners, it runs from Conyngham

Road in the west to Mount Street Bridge in the east. The road is parallel to the Grand Canal for much of its course, its eastern portions being named Harrington Street, Harcourt Road, Adelaide Road, Wilton Terrace, Herbert Place and Warrington Place.

Called South Circular Road in 1773

SOUTH EARL STREET *see* Earl Street, South

SOUTH GREAT GEORGE'S STREET
off Dame Street

After a church dedicated to St George, mentioned in 1233. Recorded as St George's Lane in 1280.

An important thoroughfare and shopping street. Built primarily by the Pim family in the 1850s; the department store of Pim Brothers dominated the street until demolition in 1970.

Called South Great George's Street in 1850

SOUTH KING STREET *see* King Street, South

SOUTH WILLIAM STREET *see* William Street, South

SPITALFIELDS
off Francis Street

After the Spitalfields in London, the centre of the English silk-weaving industry. The Dublin Spitalfields were developed deliberately to promote a domestic industry; Huguenot silk weavers were enticed here and for a time they prospered. The coming of long trousers, which made knee-length silk sockings superfluous, ruined them though poplin (a mixture of silk and wool) remained highly prized for men's ties. 'Spital' is a shortened form of 'hospital'.

Called Spitalfields in 1756

See also Parliament Street

STONEYBATTER
joins Blackhall Place

From the Irish *bóthar na gcloch* meaning the 'road of stones'. The word 'batter' usually indicates an ancient road. Almost certainly it marks the route of the ancient Gaelic road, Slige Cualann, running from south Leinster via the hurdle ford of Áth Cliath to Tara and beyond.

Called Stoneybatter in 1603

See also Drury Street

SUFFOLK STREET
off Grafton Street

The Thingmote stood close by here.

Called Suffolk Street in 1728

See also St Andrew's Street

SWIFT'S ALLEY
off Francis Street

After Dean Jonathan Swift's nephew, Thomas Swift, son-in-law to Sir Humphrey Jervis.

Called Swift's Alley in 1728

See also Jervis Street

TALBOT STREET
off Amiens Street

After Charles Chetwynd Talbot, 2nd Earl of

Talbot, Lord Lieutenant 1817–21. Formerly Cope Street North, 1795.

Seán Treacy, who with Dan Breen had begun the Anglo-Irish War at Soloheadbeg in January 1919, was cornered and killed here in 1920:

> Our lovely Seán is dead and gone,
> Shot down in Talbot Street.

A similar ballad was not composed for the British agent who died almost simultaneously from Treacy's last shot.

Called Talbot Street in 1821

TARA STREET
off Townsend Street

After the ancient seat of the High Kings. In 1766 it was Stocking Lane which appears in the early nineteenth century as Shoe Lane. Engines from the fire station here rushed north on the night of Easter Tuesday 1941 to tackle fires raging in Belfast after the first major German air raid. Many a Dubliner learned to swim in the public baths here.

Called Tara Street in 1885

TEMPLE BAR
off Fleet Street

After the Temple family, forebears of Prime Minister Lord Palmerston, whose house and gardens were here. Sir William Temple, the first member of the family to live in Dublin, was Provost of Trinity College in 1609. The name is also a reminder of the London street.

Called Temple Bar in 1707

See also Temple Lane *and* Temple Street, North

TEMPLE LANE
off Dame Street

After the Temple family. Formerly Dirty Lane, first recorded in 1728, and originally Hogges Lane after the nearby Hoggen Green.

Called Temple Lane in 1756

See also College Green *and* Temple Bar

TEMPLE STREET, NORTH
joins Hill Street

After the Temple family. It included Hill Street until 1886.

Called Temple Street, North in 1773

See also Hill Street *and* Temple Bar

TENTERFIELDS

Where cloth was stretched and dried on contraptions called tenters by means of hooks (hence, 'to be on tenterhooks' when one is in a state of tension). This area was the centre of the woollen-weaving trade in the eighteenth and early nineteenth centuries. The weavers became destitute after the Union, being unable to compete with Leeds and Halifax. In 1815 Thomas Pleasants built them a Stove Tenter House in Brown Street to enable them to dry their cloth under shelter and to work through the winter. The industry, however, was doomed.

In maps of 1800–29 the Tenterfields are

marked as lying between Marrowbone Lane and Cork Street

Called Tenterfields in the early nineteenth century

See also The Coombe, Cork Street, Marrowbone Lane *and* Weaver's Square

THOMAS STREET
joins James's Street

After the Church of St Thomas founded by William Fitz Aldelm in 1175 at the behest of Henry II – probably to atone for his part in the murder of Thomas à Becket. It runs along the line of the ancient highway, the Slige Mhór.

In medieval times this street ran from New Gate west to St James's Gate and the city's water supply was taken down it through a narrow pipe. 'Silken Thomas' Fitzgerald took his army up this street from Co. Kildare to make an assault on the city in 1534 only to be repelled by the apprentices at New Gate. In 1798 Silken Thomas's descendant, Lord Edward Fitzgerald, leader of the United Irishmen, was mortally wounded while resisting arrest in the house of Murphy the feather merchant where he was recuperating from influenza. In 1803 the Robert Emmet insurrection came to grief here but not before the Chief Justice Lord Kilwarden and his nephew had been pulled from their coach and piked to death by the insurgents.

Called Thomas Street in 1263

See also Lord Edward Street

TOWNSEND STREET
off Hawkins Street

Marked the end of the town before reclamation of tidal mud. The Long Stone stood here.

Called Townsend Street in 1674

See also D'Olier Street *and* Hawkins Street

USHER STREET
off Usher's Quay

After the Ussher family. Originally Dog and Duck Yard from a tavern situated here in 1709.

Called Usher Street in 1756

See also Bridgefoot Street, Usher's Island *and* Usher's Quay

USHER'S ISLAND

Originally an island created by the River Camac, one branch of which turned northwards at Bloody Bridge (now Rory O'More Bridge) while the other continued eastwards some distance before emptying into an inlet of the River Liffey known as Usher's Pill near the town house of the Ussher family. In 1683 the eastern branch of the Camac was dammed and Bridgefoot Street laid out and Arran Bridge erected. The island was no more but the name was retained.

Called after the Old English family of Ussher, long associated with the city. John Ussher was Mayor of Dublin in 1574; he had his rent for the island rebated 'for his changes done and bestowed upon The island. . . which island is bewest the bridge of the city of Dublin'. James

Ussher became the Protestant Archbishop of Armagh in 1625 and was later professor of divinity at Trinity College, a noted historian and prolific writer who donated his great book collection to the university. The Revd Henry Ussher was the first astronomer appointed to Dunsink Observatory, opened in 1786.

Called Usher's Island in 1562

See also Bridgefoot Street, Island Street *and* Usher's Quay

BARRACK AND QUEEN'S BRIDGES

USHER'S QUAY

After the Ussher family. The Dublin Corporation leased the area to John Ussher in 1597. Both he and Sir William Ussher had houses nearby.

Called Usher's Quay in 1728

See also Bridgefoot Street, Usher's Island *and* Usher Street

VICTORIA QUAY

After Queen Victoria, who made four state visits to Dublin in 1849, 1853, 1861 and 1900. During the second visit made to see Dargan's exhibition, the queen, as she was driven through the city, delighted the watching crowd by pulling off her son Prince Alfred's hat and giving him a hearty slap across the cheek for some youthful misdemeanour. The opposite quay (renamed Wolfe Tone Quay this century) on the north side of the river was originally Albert Quay after her beloved consort.

Called Victoria Quay in 1861

See also Wolfe Tone Quay

WATERFORD STREET
off Marlborough Street

After the Earl of Tyrone (1735–1800) who was created Marquis of Waterford in 1789 and whose residence was nearby. First recorded in 1765, it was named Mecklinburgh Street to celebrate George III's marriage to Princess Charlotte of Mecklinburgh-Strelitz. Its lower end became the heart of 'Monto', Dublin's red-light district. The Dublin Corporation attempted to change its character by renaming it Tyrone Street in 1886. Its disreputable trade persisted, however, and is attested to by the brothels, particularly Circe's palace, depicted there in James Joyce's *Ulysses*. The lower end was renamed Railway Street in 1911, while the upper end retained the connection with the Tyrone family.

Called Waterford Street in 1911

See also Foley Street, Marlborough Street *and* Railway Street

WATLING STREET
off Usher's Island

After London's Watling Street

Called Watling Street in 1766

WEAVER'S SQUARE
joins Ormond Street

After the hand-loom weavers who worked in their homes and were praised by Dean Jonathan Swift:

> We'll dress in manufactures made at home,
> Equip our kings and generals in the Coombe.

Called Weaver's Square in 1758

See also The Coombe *and* Tenterfields

WELLINGTON QUAY

After Arthur Wellesley, Duke of Wellington, who defeated Napoleon at Waterloo in 1815. Formerly called Customhouse Quay after the old Custom House which stood here 1621–1791.

Called Wellington Quay in 1817

See also Grafton Street

WERBURGH STREET
off Castle Street

After St Werburgh's Church founded on the site of the ancient Church of St Martin and named in the early thirteenth century after the English saint. The church was rebuilt in 1662, again in 1759, and given a spire and a tower in 1768. The spire and tower were demolished in 1836 for fear that insurgents would use it for an attack on Dublin Castle. Lord Edward Fitzgerald, the insurrectionary leader of 1798, is buried in the vaults.

New Theatre, Dublin's first professional theatre, was opened here in 1637. Jonathan Swift was born close to the church in Hoey's Court in 1667.

Called Werburgh Street in 1257

See also Lord Edward Street

WESTLAND ROW
off Pearse Street

After William Westland who owned property here. In December 1834 the first steam locomotive in Ireland pulled out of the station named after the street (now Pearse Station). Oscar Wilde was born at number 21.

Called Westland Row in 1776

WESTMORELAND STREET
off College Green

After John Fane, 10th Earl of Westmorland, Lord Lieutenant 1790–95. He promoted measures of Catholic relief in the Irish Parliament but baulked at supporting full Catholic emancipation. Laid out around 1800 by the Wide Street Commissioners, its principal building, number 21, was the Ballast Office; erected in 1802 by the Corporation for Preserving and Improving the Port of Dublin, this imposing office, with its clock regulated

EAST FRONT OF THE BANK OF IRELAND

from Dunsink Observatory, was for long a notable landmark but it was demolished in 1979.

Called Westmoreland Street in 1801

WEXFORD STREET
joins Camden Street

Possibly after the county. Formerly Kevin's Port after St Kevin's Gate which led into the Liberty of St Sepulchre.

Called Wexford Street in 1839

WHITEFRIARS STREET
off Aungier Street

The name retains the memory of the medieval Whitefriars Lane which followed the route of the modern Camden Street, Wexford Street, Redmond's Hill, Whitefriars Street and went on to meet Golden Lane and Ship Street. Called after the Carmelite or Whitefriars' Monastery, built by Sir Robert Bagod in 1278, dissolved in 1539 and re-established in 1825.

Called Whitefriars Street in 1871

See also Baggot Street

WICKLOW STREET
off Grafton Street

Possibly after the county. Originally included in Exchequer Street.

Called Wicklow Street in 1839

POWERSCOURT HOUSE

WILLIAM STREET, SOUTH
off Wicklow Street

After William III, victor of the Battle of the Boyne 1690. Dominated by Powerscourt House, built in 1771 for Richard Wingfield, 3rd Viscount Powerscourt. The mansion is almost disproportionately tall and grand for an inner-city street. Sold (like so many other aristocratic town houses after the Union) to the Commissioners of Stamp Duties in 1807 and then to a drapery firm, it has blossomed in recent years as a new shopping and social centre. The Civic Museum is nearby.

Called William Street, South in the 1690s

WINETAVERN STREET
off Wood Quay

After the wine and ale merchants concentrated here. Also referred to as Taverners' Street and

BRIDGE CONNECTING CHRIST CHURCH WITH THE SYNOD HALL

one of the principal streets of early Dublin. The present street has been widened and incorporates the original Michael's Hill, previously Christchurch Lane. Excavations in the 1960s uncovered remarkable Norse and medieval material, including over 2,000 engraved pewter tokens, probably used to pay for drinks in Winetavern Street.

The earliest city wall ran across what would now be the middle of the street where it was pierced by Winetavern or King's Gate. Later, after much of the foreshore had been reclaimed, Prickett's Tower stood at the bottom of the street. The Crane, where imported goods were weighed and duty paid, operated just west of the tower. Here, on 11 March 1597, around 14,000 lb of gunpowder accidentally exploded; as Sir John Norris reported: '. . . the keper of the Crane, and all the labourers about yt are peryshed: the ruyne of the town is exceedinge great. . .' A committee of inquiry concluded that the number of people lost came to 'six skoare, besides sondrie headles bodies, and heades without bodies that were found and not knowne. . .'

In the seventeenth century the Royal Exchange

stood here and every other house was a tavern. Barnaby Rych denounced the ale sold there as 'hogges wash' sold by women who were 'both verie loathsome, filthie and abominable'. The street dropped rapidly down the social scale in the nineteenth century except for the Irish House, a public house at the corner of Wood Quay extravagantly decorated in the Celtic Revival style. It was from this corner that the Irish Civil War began on the morning of 28 June 1922 when a field gun of the National Army shelled the Four Courts occupied by the Irregulars. Demolition of the decayed houses in the street began in the 1960s.

Called Winetavern Street in the thirteenth century

See also Wood Quay

WOLFE TONE QUAY

After Theobald Wolfe Tone, who helped to found the United Irishmen in 1791 and negotiated the French expedition to Bantry Bay in 1796. Captured on board a French vessel off Donegal in 1798, he took his own life in his cell while awaiting execution. Originally called Albert Quay.

Called Wolfe Tone Quay in 1933

See also Victoria Quay

WOOD QUAY

After an extensive timber revetment driven into the tidal mud to create an anchorage in the thirteenth century.

This is Dublin's oldest quay and behind it – in an area bounded by Christ Church, Fishamble Street and Winetavern Street – some of the best preserved and most impressive Viking remains in all of Europe, together with material from Norman Dublin, were excavated in the 1970s. Finds included: wattlework fences, paths and dwellings; tanning pits and cesspits; tanged knives, scoops, spoons, ladles, anvils, hammers, axes, boring bits, tongs, shears and other implements; board games, model wooden boats and bone whistles for children; hundreds of fine combs for removing lice; and pieces of cloth, leather and remains of severed heads; a babe in its mother's arms and a tenth-century pet terrier.

Sir Henry Sydney, Queen Elizabeth's Lord Deputy, departed from here in 1578. The first book to be printed in Ireland, the Book of Common Prayer, was 'Imprinted by Humfrey Powell, Printer to the Kynges Maiestie' in Prickett's Tower on the junction between Merchants' Quay and Wood Quay in 1551. In the seventeenth century men of property and fashion had houses on the quay including Viscount Loftus, Francis Aungier, Baron Longford, and Sir Faithful Fortescue, ancestor of the Earls of Clermont. The quay's standing declined as trade moved downriver and by the mid-nineteenth century it was a place of shops, craftsmen and grim tenements. By the mid-1960s the houses and business premises were due for demolition.

The discovery of priceless archaeological

remains coincided with the corporation's scheme to build its new offices behind Wood Quay. Despite a tenacious campaign to preserve the historic site – which included massive demonstrations, an occupation known as Operation Sitric and pleas from scholars across the world – the area was covered over with cement and massive tower blocks erected. An opportunity to mount an exhibition to rival Jorvik in York was thereby lost.

Called Wood Quay in the thirteenth century

See also Winetavern Street

YARNHALL STREET
off Bolton Street

After the nearby Yarn Hall. Built for the sale of linen yarn, it is now incorporated in the Bolton Street Technical College.

Called Yarnhall Street in 1800

See also Linenhall Street

YORK STREET
off St Stephen's Green

After the Duke of York 1674–1728, Earl of Ulster and brother of George I.

Called York Street in 1728

O'CONNELL BRIDGE

BRIDGES OF DUBLIN

Even before the city was founded the great highways of ancient Ireland converged at the hurdle-ford crossing of the River Liffey. The Vikings built the first bridge close by but others did not follow until Sir Humphrey Jervis began developing the city north of the river in the seventeenth century.

The bridges described below are taken from west to east.

ISLAND BRIDGE

After an island on the Liffey. First named Sarah Bridge after Sarah Fane, Countess Westmorland, who laid the foundation stone in 1791. The name did not stick, however, as citizens preferred to call it either Kilmainham Bridge or Island Bridge. Renamed Island Bridge in 1922.

SEÁN HEUSTON BRIDGE

After the insurgent leader who was executed after the Easter Rising, 1916. Built in 1828 as

SEÁN HEUSTON BRIDGE

King's Bridge and named to commemorate the royal visit of George IV in 1821. Renamed Sarsfield Bridge in 1922, it was renamed again as Seán Heuston Bridge in 1941.

FRANK SHERWIN BRIDGE

After a popular councillor who died in 1981. Opened in 1982.

RORY O'MORE BRIDGE

After the leader of the 1641 insurrection. Bloody Bridge was erected here in the seventeenth century and acquired its name from a riot there in 1671. Replaced by the stone Barrack Bridge in the eighteenth century (being next to the Royal Barracks, for a time the largest in the British Empire), rebuilt as Victoria Bridge in 1863 and renamed again as Rory O'More Bridge in 1922.

LIAM MELLOWS BRIDGE

After the republican leader who was executed by the Free State Government in 1922. The oldest bridge still spanning the Liffey, it has had many names: Arran Bridge, Bridewell

Bridge, Ellis's Bridge, Queen Maev Bridge. Renamed Liam Mellows Bridge in 1942.

FATHER MATTHEW BRIDGE

After the nineteenth century temperance reformer. Built in 1818, it was first named Whitworth Bridge after Charles Whitworth, 1st Earl of Whitworth, Lord Lieutenant 1813–17. This is on or near the site of the Old Bridge erected early in the thirteenth century to replace the Viking bridge known as Dubhghall's Bridge. Renamed Dublin Bridge in 1922 and renamed again as Father Matthew Bridge *c.* 1938.

O'DONOVAN ROSSA BRIDGE

After the Fenian Brotherhood leader who died in 1915. Built in 1818 and named Richmond Bridge after Charles Lennox, 4th Duke of Richmond, Lord Lieutenant 1807–13. Replaced the seventeenth-century Ormonde Bridge. Renamed O'Donovan Rossa Bridge in 1922.

GRATTAN BRIDGE

After the leader of the Patriot Party in the Irish House of Commons 1776–1800. Erected in 1676 and named Essex Bridge after Arthur Capel, Earl of Essex, Lord Lieutenant 1672–7. Rebuilt and renamed Grattan Bridge in 1875.

LIFFEY BRIDGE

Erected in 1816 and named Wellington Bridge, it was one of the first half-dozen cast-iron bridges in the world. Popularly known as the

Halfpenny Bridge, after the toll charge which ceased to be levied in 1919. Renamed Liffey Bridge in 1922.

O'CONNELL BRIDGE

O'CONNELL BRIDGE

After Daniel O'Connell, the leader of the Catholic Emancipation and Repeal movements. Completed in 1794 it became the principal crossing over the Liffey. First named Carlisle Bridge after Frederick Howard, 5th Earl of Carlisle, Lord Lieutenant 1780–82. Widened and renamed O'Connell Bridge in 1880.

BUTT BRIDGE

After Isaac Butt, founder of the nineteenth-century Home Rule movement. Built in 1878 and twice rebuilt in 1904 and 1932.

THE LOOP LINE RAILWAY BRIDGE

Erected in 1891, this bridge is so ugly that it has never been thought fitting to name it after anyone. It blocks the view of the Custom House from O'Connell Bridge.

TALBOT MEMORIAL BRIDGE

After Matt Talbot, who quit a life of drunken squalor for one of saintly self-mortification. Erected and named in 1978.

BIBLIOGRAPHY

Bardon, Jonathan and Stephen Conlin. *Dublin: One Thousand Years of Wood Quay*, Blackstaff Press, 1984

Brooking, Charles. *A Map of the City and Suburbs of Dublin*, London, 1728

Clarke, Howard B. *Dublin c 840–c 1540: The Medieval Town in the Modern City*, The Friends of Medieval Dublin and the Ordnance Survey, 1978

'The topographical development of early medieval Dublin', *Journal of the Royal Society of Antiquaries of Ireland*, vol. 107 (1977)

Daly, Mary. *Dublin: The Deposed Capital. A Social and Economic History 1860–1914*, Cork University Press, 1984

The Dublin Historical Record, 41 vols. (1939–)

Gilbert, J.T. *History of Dublin*, 3 vols., James Duffy, 1861

Gilbert, J.T. and R.M. Gilbert (eds.). *Calendar of Ancient Records of Dublin in Possession of the Municipal Corporation of that City*, 19 vols., Joseph Dollard, 1889–1944

Gillespie, Elgy (ed.). *The Liberties of Dublin*, O'Brien Press, 1973

Granville, Gary (ed.). *Divided City: Portrait of Dublin 1913*, Curriculum Development Unit, O'Brien Press, 1978

Haliday, Charles. *The Scandinavian Kingdom of Dublin*, Alex Thom, 1881

Harte, Frank (ed.). *Songs of Dublin*, Gilbert Dalton, 1978

Kiely, Benedict (ed.). *Dublin*, Oxford University Press, 1983

Killanin, Lord and Michael V. Duignan. *The Shell Guide to Ireland*, Ebury Press, 1962

MacLoughlin, Adrian. *Guide to Historic Dublin*, Gill & Macmillan, 1979

Mac Thomáis, Eamonn. *Me Jewel and Darlin' Dublin*, O'Brien Press, 1974

Maxwell, Constantia. *Dublin Under the Georges 1714–1830*, Harrap, 1936

McCready, C.T. *Dublin Street Names Dated and Explained*, Gibbs, 1892

Moody, T.W., F.X. Martin and F.J. Byrne (eds.) *A New History of Ireland IX: Maps, Genealogies, Lists: A Companion to Irish History. Part II*, Oxford University Press, 1982

O'Dwyer, Frederick. *Lost Dublin*, Gill & Macmillan, 1981

Rocque, John. *An Exact Survey of the City and Suburbs of Dublin*, 1756 (map)

Somerville-Large, Peter. *Dublin*, Hamish Hamilton, 1979

Stanihurst, Richard. 'Description of Dublin 1577', in *Holinshed's Irish Chronicle, 1577*, Dolmen Press edition, 1979

Thom's Official Directory of Great Britain and Ireland, together with the Post Office Directory of Dublin and Suburbs, Alex Thom, (1844–)

ACKNOWLEDGEMENT

Grateful acknowledgement is made to Katherine B. Kavanagh, c/o Peter Fallon, 19 Oakdown Road, Dublin 14, for permission to quote from 'If Ever You Go To Dublin Town' by Patrick Kavanagh.